ANGELS
IN THE
FIRE

ANGELS
IN THE
FIRE

THE DRAMATIC TRUE STORY
of an IMPOSSIBLE RESCUE

DANN STADLER

BETHANYHOUSE
a division of Baker Publishing Group
Minneapolis, Minnesota

© 2013 by Daniel J. Stadler

Published by Bethany House Publishers
11400 Hampshire Avenue South
Bloomington, Minnesota 55438
www.bethanyhouse.com

Bethany House Publishers is a division of
Baker Publishing Group, Grand Rapids, Michigan

Printed in the United States of America

Library of Congress Cataloging-in-Publication Data
Stadler, Dann.
    Angels in the fire : the dramatic true story of an impossible rescue / Dann Stadler.
        pages cm
    ISBN 978-0-7642-1114-0 (pbk. : alk. paper)
    1. Burns and scalds—Patients—Biography. 2. Burns and scalds—Religious aspects—Christianity. 3. Crash injuries—Patients—Religious life. 4. Providence and government of God—Christianity. I. Title.
RD96.4.S73 2013
617.1′1—dc23   2013007776

Some names of persons in this account have been changed to protect their privacy.

Cover design by Gearbox

Author is represented by The Seymour Agency

13 14 15 16 17 18 19   7 6 5 4 3 2 1

For Tracey
We've been through so much and I have asked
so much of you, yet you've stood with me—
twenty-seven years—no small task
The ways you look at me, talk to me,
and through your gentle touch,
you silently repeat your vows to me every day
I am awed you said "I do" just once

For our daughters, Meghan, Rebekah, and Emma
You are the shining stars who believe in us no matter
what and scatter light throughout our lives

For Tracey's parents
Though no longer with us, your supportive
echoes stayed with me as I wrote these pages

For my parents
Your belief in us and support have been a
rock in the shifting sands of our lives

Contents

Contents

1

Highway to ~~Hell~~ Heaven

It's 8 p.m., Thursday, September 7, 1989, and Mark Payne* is finishing the day at his father's car dealership in Riviera Beach, Florida. He's hungry and wants something to eat. However, what he really craves is something to drink, not merely to slake his thirst but to satisfy his urgent need to flood his brain and body with numbing spirits.

He stops at a nearby restaurant and orders his first drink. By his last glass of whiskey, just before midnight, he's forgotten about his hunger. His goal for the night is satisfied—his mind is numbed, his senses are dulled. Despite his unsteady

*Not his real name. There is no need to cite the name of the drunk driver who hit us that night. It is a matter of public record, if anyone cares to know. I feel that using his real name would only be an act of vengeance and is unnecessary.

walk and failing several times to get his key in the car door, he crumples his body into the driver's seat, cranks the engine to life, and heads home, some ten miles north. When he reaches the on-ramp to I-95 North, he briefly thinks about his last arrest, a DUI some seven months ago, and hopes he won't pass any troopers on the way. With just a few miles to go, he laughs off the risk and puts his Grateful Dead tape in, blasting the music.

Payne travels nearly thirty miles past the exit to his home in Jupiter. Somehow realizing the mistake through his alcoholic haze, he knows he has to head back south. Thinking he's on the two-lane road that he usually takes home, he pulls his car over to the right shoulder, waits for the other cars to pass, and makes a wide U-turn. Knowing his wife might worry about him being so late, he steps on the gas and cruises along at 70 miles per hour.

Payne has no idea that he is now traveling the wrong way, heading south on the far right side of the northbound lanes on the six-lane divided freeway of I-95. He has U-turned himself and his red BMW into an unguided missile. The Grateful Dead keep pounding in his ears. It is the last thing he will ever hear.

Dann and Tracey Stadler are driving the same stretch of road that night, returning from their fourth-anniversary dinner to Tracey's parents' house in Port St. Lucie, Florida, where they are vacationing from their home in Wisconsin.

Florida State Trooper Sydney Wright is also on I-95 that night, patrolling the freeway. Now just after midnight, she is about ten miles north of Port St. Lucie, traveling southbound when the first call comes over the radio from dispatch: "Red vehicle seen traveling southbound in the northbound lanes, just past Midway Road." It is about twenty miles south of her location.

Maybe it's a mistake, Wright thinks. *It's easy to get confused on the dark roads and see headlights that seem to come from the wrong side of the road.* Still, her stomach tightens—she's seen far too many crashes caused by wrong-way drivers. The CB radio crackles with the rough voice of a trucker. He too reports a small red car going the wrong way. A few minutes later the dispatcher comes on with yet another report. With her sirens wailing and lights flashing, Trooper Wright accelerates through the darkness.

At 12:35 a.m. the final call comes in: "Accident with injuries reported, I-95 North, mile marker 109, two miles south of County Road 714. Vehicle fire reported." Wright's adrenaline surges and her heart sinks. *Oh no. He got someone.*

The sudden impact between the two cars sends a bright fireball over the highway, surely seen by every driver within half a mile. Just as quickly, the fireball evaporates and leaves a flickering hulk of twisted metal in its place on the road, the two cars now crumpled to almost half their original size and standing just inches apart. Almost a dozen cars come to an abrupt halt and some of the occupants race toward the smoldering masses of metal. Fear rips through the night air. *There is no way anyone could survive a crash that horrific.* Troy Lynne reaches the cars first; the driver of the red BMW is clearly dead. Lynne looks at the other car, which is still burning. Incredibly, both people inside are stirring—alive!

He tries to open the doors, but they won't budge. The front end of the car is pushed in more than four feet; the doors are jammed shut. Lynne can see the flames stabbing at the driver's legs. He waves frantically toward the horde coming upon the scene, shouting for a fire extinguisher.

I have no recollection of that night following my admonition to Tracey to keep her seat belt on. Tracey doesn't recall the actual crash, as she was likely sleeping, but the rest of her memories are terrifying—save for an all too brief divine interlude.

After our violent impact, Tracey could only look at me in confusion, silently imploring *What happened?* I stared back. Then I reached over to try to unbuckle our seat belts. It was too much for Tracey to comprehend. *Am I dreaming?*

The screams outside the car brought her back to reality. As she told me later, her brain could not process anything—how the accident happened, where we were, how badly we'd been hurt, the extent of the damage, or even our names. Her head was swimming with incredible pain and dizzying thoughts. She could see flames licking at my legs and heard me scream.

Other vehicles began coming upon the wreck. The second shift of a nearby factory had just ended, and a trio of men in one vehicle moved into action. They were Mike Debevec, Ben Williams, and Kyle Longwell. As they raced to the scene with a co-worker, Mike Walters, some grabbed fire extinguishers, but nothing seemed to calm the flames. Gas was gushing in spurts from beneath our Ford sedan, and with every surge a loud *whoosh* erupted as it hit the pavement and ignited.

Lynne and others tried to pull Tracey out through a small opening between the sunroof and window, but it was as though they were trying to lift the entire car with her. Everything from the bumper in had collapsed on Tracey's lower body. She screamed as her rescuers tried to move her amid the intensifying heat.

As Lynne and others continued to try to extract Tracey, Debevec realized I had caught fire and ran to my side of the car with Walters and Longwell. They tried to force open my door without success, so they pounded the window with their fists and rocks, but it seemed to resist every blow.

In an act of incredible strength, Debevec curled his fingertips into the space between the top of the driver's-side window frame and the car. Nearly climbing onto the car door, he pulled with every ounce of strength he could muster. Meanwhile, the flames inside were creeping up my legs. The window frame suddenly yielded, and as he peeled it back, the window shattered. A searing wind shot through the opening and pushed them back.

I raised my arms, grabbed the roof of the car, and pulled myself up through the opening. Debevec, Walters, and Longwell ran back to the car, grabbed me under my arms, and pulled me from the wreck, smothering the flames with their hands.

"Get my wife out!" I shouted. I didn't call her by name; I doubt I even knew my own name. Others were still frantically trying to pull Tracey out. Another rescuer, James Vellum, reached through the hole in the roof, but still felt resistance as he tugged. I could hear her scream, and then the crowd began to panic. Vellum tried using a two-by-four someone handed him to pry open the door, but it snapped in two. The flames continued to grow more intense. Another man tried breaking the window with a spent fire extinguisher, but that attempt failed as well. With every swing it just bounced stubbornly off of the window.

Flames now filled the car and pinned Tracey against the window. The rescuers seemed powerless to help, and the crowd backed away, fearing an explosion. In the midst of this confusion and horror, a woman in the crowd sank to her knees on the pavement and began to pray—pleading with God to help the rescuers. As she prayed, Pedro Gimenez saw a silent lone figure walk out of the woods. The glow of the fire grew brighter against his face as he drew closer to the car.

But as Gimenez watched, it became clear that the glow was not a reflection of the car fire—it was emanating *from* the figure. Gimenez knew then that the man was not just another spectator who'd happened upon the scene. He was seeing . . . an angel.

At that moment, Ben Williams, who had been riding with Debevec and Longwell, helped the only way he could think of—he began to pray for hope and healing. He later described it: "As I stood in the middle of the road that night with all the activity and confusion going on around me, I just kept praying. Then I suddenly felt an intense rush come over me. I felt the healing power of Jesus Christ so strongly, so intensely, and so overwhelmingly that I just buckled to my knees on the pavement and I couldn't get back up. I knew the Lord was healing the people in that car. It was a wonderful, incredible feeling; I just sat there on the pavement in awe."

Tracey looked at the horrified faces surrounding the car. She locked eyes with one woman who was crying. The searing heat sucked her breath away; her lungs felt as if they would burst from within. Then Tracey could feel and smell the flesh on her face burning. *Please, God,* she prayed, *take me now before I burn to death.*

An instant later she looked up and saw an incredible sight—Jesus was reaching out to her. At that moment Tracey seemed to float to heaven, just as Longwell was able to remove her lifeless body from the car.

Here is Tracey's story in her own words:

After Dann and I went out for our fourth anniversary that night, I remember waving good-bye to my brother Tommy after we reached I-95. I told Dann I was going to take a nap on the way home. The last thing I remember was him telling me to keep my seat belt on, which I did.

My next memory was of intense pain. I recall seeing and hearing people yelling and screaming outside our car windows. I thought I was dreaming, but quickly realized this was no dream. I turned my head and looked at Dann. I can still see him, both of us with helpless expressions. He tried to unbuckle our seat belts and then began to scream. I looked down at his legs and realized he was on fire. I tried to get to him, but could not move because the dash and the engine were pressing against my legs. Everything below my waist had been crushed. I started screaming and realized my jaw was broken. When I opened my mouth, I could feel my chin moving against my earlobe. That's when I realized how hurt I was.

The flames engulfed Dann. I can't begin to explain the horror of seeing him burning. I was pinned against my seat and the door, and I couldn't reach him. Just when it looked as though he would be completely overtaken by the flames, someone peeled open his window. Others helped pull him out of the car. I was glad he was out, but I thought he was

15

dead. Someone tried to get my door open, but it didn't work. He tried again to pull me out through the sunroof. Still I wouldn't budge; I was trapped. Then everyone began to back away because the heat and flames were too intense. I heard people screaming and yelling to get away; the car was going to blow up. I was hysterical. *My God, they're going to leave me here to burn to death!*

I could feel the flames getting closer and closer and my face and arms begin to burn. It was so hot. My lungs and chest felt like they were on fire. I couldn't breathe. I began to pray with all the energy I had left. I can still recall the prayer: *"God, please forgive me for my sins. You said that you have many mansions—I pray that there is room for me in heaven. I also pray that you take me now so I don't burn to death. Please don't let me burn."*

In the next instant, I looked up and saw Him—Jesus—my Lord and Savior. He looked almost like an angel to me, but I knew it was Him. I felt like He was there to comfort me and to heal me. Throughout my experience, He was with me. I felt like I'd known Him my entire life, even though we had never "met" before.

I wondered how many other times He must have been there for me when I needed help. My mind was racing—how did I know Him? I just knew that somehow our paths had crossed, that we were connected. I wanted to talk to Him but found we didn't have to speak words. We communicated through our minds. As He reached toward me, my first "words" to Him were, "Boy, you cut this one close!" He smiled and picked me up like a parent carries a child.

The next feeling I had was that we were going "up"; He was carrying me away from the wreck. I suddenly realized what was happening. "I'm dead, aren't I?" Again, He smiled.

I was so excited and expressed to Him, "I was always afraid to die—afraid of the unknown, the pain—but this is wonderful. You should tell people about this, they need to know!" He just smiled a smile of pure beauty and truth. He told me I could look down, but I didn't want to. As we got further away from the crash site, I felt more peace. It was wonderful. In fact, it was more than I can explain. It wasn't just escaping the pain of the crash, I was leaving behind every physical pain I had ever had, every emotional trauma I had ever experienced. The heaviness of my earthly body melted away. Even the burden of what had been my life on earth seemed, in His presence, to turn into an airy lightness of pure freedom and joy.

I was vaguely aware of scenes of my life all around me. All the good memories flashed by me but I wasn't paying attention because I was so focused on Jesus. I wasn't just overwhelmed; I was consumed by His love, by His complete and utter peace. It was more than amazing.

The words that kept repeating in my mind were from a passage in the Bible: "the peace that passes all understanding." I felt this incredible, indescribable peace that was all-encompassing—but it wasn't just a feeling, it became part of who I was. I *became* peace, love, and joy. All these intense feelings came from Jesus and cannot be properly explained. It was overwhelming. It was wonderful. It was indescribable—how intense these feelings and this reality were. The love that a parent feels for a child is one of the strongest loves there is, but even that pales in comparison with His love. I felt like His arms were wrapped around me, holding me and making me feel completely and perfectly loved. I can't describe it any other way.

As we went further, I felt as if I were finally going home. I knew with my whole heart and to the depths of my soul that God, our Father, was waiting for me. Think about that, He was waiting—for me! There was no pain, no sadness, no regret, only pure anticipation—like this was what "perfect" was, what everything in life, everything I had ever known, was all about. It was like I was being born again into a perfect and pure world. I realized death is not the opposite of life, it is the opposite of birth, and here I was—ready to meet God, fully alive and fully loved. I was so excited. And I knew there was one reason, and one reason only, I was going to heaven—because I had known Jesus and chosen Him as my Savior during my life on earth. That is all that mattered. I cannot emphasize that enough—all of my life, every decision, every action, every question—everything that I was, all came down to that one decision. Nothing else mattered, nothing—it was Christ and Christ alone.

I looked up again, or maybe I became more aware of where I was, and I suddenly saw my grandmother, Nannie, who had died when I was only six months old. I didn't see her in human form, yet I immediately recognized her. She was a presence of great warmth and endless love. I never knew her in my life, but felt that somehow she had always been with me, as if there were some sort of lifelong bond that I only now understood. She was waiting at the entrance to heaven to take me in and was clearly thrilled to see me. I felt pure joy radiating from her. I looked at her and just shouted an excited, "Nannie!" I could not wait to be with her. Her presence was so loving and welcoming that I felt like I almost melted into her.

Just as I reached her, thoughts of my daughter, Meghan, who was only nine months old, suddenly filled my mind. I cried out her name. I began to panic, as I thought that Dann had died. I just felt so strongly that Meghan needed a mother;

she needed me—I didn't want her to be an orphan. I told Jesus and Nannie that I could not leave Meghan. I really wanted to go to heaven and start my new life—I wanted to feel all of God, all of His love and peace—but I couldn't leave my baby.

Nannie and Jesus became intensely serious. I knew I had to make a choice—and I had no time to dwell on it, it had to be instantaneous. Although every part of my soul seemed to yearn for God, something in me made me want to go back to Meghan. I just had to be her mother. I felt like the only reason I could go back was for love—my love for Meghan was so strong that somehow Jesus recognized that, and even more, He honored it by allowing me the choice to return.

In the next instant I left Nannie, and Jesus began to take me back toward the scene of the wreck. Everything seemed almost as if it was a rewind of when I left the crash to go to heaven. The closer we got to earth, the heavier I felt. I had more and more pain, and my entire being felt worse. My Nannie's warmth disappeared, and I felt cold. When the pain became intense, I suddenly knew I was back—"alive" again, back on earth.

When I came back to life on the side of the road, I looked up and found I was looking directly into the eyes of an angel. I knew in an instant that he was an angel—and he knew me. Somehow I knew he had saved me from dying in the burning car. Someone else physically pulled me from the car, but I know it only happened because the angel made it happen. I can't explain how, I just know. He bent over me on the road, put his hand over my face, and healed me.

Specifically, I felt that he healed the burns on my face and neck through the power of Jesus. With all of my injuries, I knew that I could not withstand burns on my face. I think God knew I could not survive with burns—He knew it was more than I could bear. I know I was burned inside the car, and I know the power of Jesus healed me through my angel. I just felt His healing power surge through me, especially on my face. Then the angel told me, "Tracey, everything is going to be all right."

As Tracey was "dying" in the car, Kyle Longwell was still trying to pull her free from the burning wreck. He reached in through the jagged hole between the door and the sunroof, and pulled her through the flames and out of the car—this time without any effort at all, as if the wreckage clutching Tracey's legs suddenly released its grip.

He later told us, "A power came down on me, a strength that couldn't have come from me." Tracey was free.

They laid her down next to the car—her injuries apparent.

After Tracey's earthly life surged through her body, and the angel told her everything would be "all right," he looked at the crowd and in slow, deliberate speech, said, "Take–care–of–Tracey." Gimenez watched as the angel returned to the woods, seemingly absorbed in the shadows.

Neither Tracey nor I, nor anyone at the scene, had spoken our names, yet the angel clearly knew hers.

2

The Longest Night

At Martin Memorial Hospital in Stuart, Florida, Dr. Belle gets a call in the ER from paramedics. It's about 12:50 a.m.— "MVA, two victims with multiple trauma and burns—it's a bad one. ETA fifteen minutes." The paramedics and doctor are well aware of "the Golden Hour," the fact that trauma victims are more likely to survive if they can get definitive life-saving care within sixty minutes.

Acutely aware of the challenges ahead with two severely injured patients, especially with burns, Dr. Belle acts quickly. The second shift has just finished and many are still in the hospital, so she directs the charge nurse, "Get the second shift back in here now. We need everyone we can get. And find every physician that's on call and tell them to come in. No questions—just get here as soon as possible."

I arrived ahead of Tracey, and the ER staff moved quickly to stabilize me. With injuries from the top of my head down to my toes, they had to assess and prioritize my injuries. Just moving me was enough to make me cry out in agony. Every touch was torture.

When Tracey arrived, she still didn't know if I was dead or alive. Despite the paramedics' reassurances, the last image she had was of me being pulled out of the car—on fire. She was sure I was dead. When the doors to the ER opened, the first thing she heard was someone screaming—it was me. She would later say those screams were "the sweetest noise I ever heard," because it meant I was still alive. A nurse met Tracey as the paramedics wheeled her in. "What's your name, honey?" Though still unable to recall her own name, from somewhere deep inside her brain, her parents' phone number came through the fog and she haltingly answered, "I don't know, but you have to call my parents . . ."

Knowing her mom and dad were on their way gave Tracey some comfort and relief—she longed to see them again. She needed their reassurance and the familiarity of their faces; she needed them to tell her that everything would be okay, and she wanted to tell them about Jesus and her angel. But she was drifting in and out of consciousness.

Earlier that night, Mary snaps awake at half past midnight with her breathing heavy and heart racing. It is as though she has awakened from a nightmare her mind cannot remember but her body still feels.

She checks on her newest granddaughter, Meghan—*Is there anything more peaceful than a sleeping baby?*—but it doesn't calm Mary's nagging concern; Dann and Tracey aren't back yet. *Where are they?* she wonders. *They should be back by now.*

We had arrived in Florida with Meghan days earlier to visit Tracey's parents, Tom and Mary, who had moved south just a few months before Meghan was born. It was a relief for Mary to see Tracey again. And though she absolutely glowed in her role as a new mother, the trip had been a reawakening for Tracey after Meghan's difficult birth. Tracey was very close to her family and missed them terribly. Her two brothers and two sisters had moved to Florida years before her mom and dad. With their departure, it was as if her entire support network had left her on her own. A bout with postpartum depression in the midst of a dark Wisconsin winter only magnified Tracey's distress.

But it was late summer now, actually September 7, 1989, and we were out celebrating our fourth anniversary with Tracey's twin brother, Tommy, and his girlfriend. And it *was* a celebration. Tracey and I were just twenty-seven years old, both college grads—I had a great job as a salesman with a pharmaceutical firm, and Tracey worked for an optometry company that would promote her to district trainer upon our return. We had a new home and a nine-month-old daughter. Meghan was a perfect baby—plump, pink, with big blue eyes and a face full of smiles.

We had every blessing life could offer and felt things could not get any better. Our careers were taking off. Tracey had recovered from her postpartum depression, shed her pregnancy pounds, and returned to her active lifestyle. I was in the best shape of my life; I ran, lifted weights, and was pursuing a black belt in Tae Kwon Do. We were healthy and happy.

———

Where are they? Mary wonders again, more anxious. She paces the house, flips through channels on the TV, checks on Meghan, again. *Still nothing.*

Mary can't get out of her mind a conversation from earlier that evening. Tracey had confided to Mary, "Mom, I have a really bad feeling about tonight; I think we should stay here." Tracey was so concerned that she was in tears. Mary just chalked it up to a nervous holdover from her recent depression, being so far from home, and leaving her baby behind for the evening. She had told her to go out and have fun. "Everything will be just fine."

———

It is now almost 1 a.m, and still no sign of them. She calls Tommy and asks when Dann and Tracey left to come home. Tommy explains that after they left the restaurant, he led them through town and pointed them toward Port St. Lucie at about 11:30 p.m. *Plenty of time for them to be back by now.*

Tommy, a West Palm Beach police officer not given to panic, reassures his mother that they will be home soon. "Mom, they probably stopped for gas, or maybe they had a flat tire. I'm sure they're fine. If they're not back in twenty or thirty minutes, call me back and I'll go out and retrace their route."

———

It had been a long day, and we were both tired, especially Tracey. She had been up early to visit with her mom and take care of Meghan. On our way home she took off her seat belt and tried to catch a little sleep. When I asked what she was doing, she explained, "This seat belt is uncomfortable when I'm lying back." My last pre-crash memory is telling her, "Well, it's a lot more uncomfortable lying in a hospital bed because you didn't have your seat belt on." She buckled up, but I had no idea how prescient my last words to her that night would be.

I can't explain why, but from a young age I always expected I would be involved in a great crisis of some sort. I was somewhat of a loner and a fighter, and being in a crash of this magnitude and left fighting for my life wasn't something I had ever really expected, but I wasn't completely shocked by it either.

Tracey's personality and upbringing are in stark contrast to mine. She grew up believing that as long as you live by the rules and are a good and decent person, the world will be peaceful and life will be wonderful—every blessing was a reward for leading a good life. She had a quintessential American upbringing, almost the living embodiment of a Norman Rockwell painting.

Born of older Depression-era parents who lived through WWII—a family of seven with two sisters several years older than her, a twin brother, and a younger brother—her life was a tapestry of sunny memories. Her mom was a nurse and her dad a WWII Navy veteran and steel salesman, both raised within sniffing distance of the smoky bitterness of Ohio's Youngstown steel mills. Tom and Mary moved from their native Ohio to Wisconsin just a few years before Tracey and Tommy were born and lived there until retiring to Florida.

My parents were quite young when I was born—just twenty-one. I was the eldest of three, with a brother a year younger and a sister three years younger. We moved almost every three years, with Mom and Dad chasing a better life. It seemed like I was always adjusting to new situations. I excelled in school, but hated every minute of it and never quite felt like I fit in. We moved for the last time the summer before my freshman year in high school, back to where we started—Germantown, Wisconsin, a small community near Milwaukee. It was a welcome return to our true hometown.

The phone rings at Mary and Tom's house. *Maybe they're calling to say their car is stalled or they have a flat tire. Maybe they're lost. Anything . . .* Mary silently pleads. But when she answers the phone, it isn't what she wants to hear. An ER nurse for over thirty years, Mary encounters an echo of the words she has said herself so many times, words she dreaded to say, much less hear in her own ear. "This is Martin Memorial Hospital in Stuart. Your daughter and her husband have been in a car accident. You need to come in as soon as you can."

Time stops. Mary's voice escapes her for a moment, until she can ask, "How are they? Are they alive?" Again, she doesn't get the reply for which she was hoping. The nurse's words are hesitant and spoken with an ever so slight cracking.

"They're alive, but they're in critical condition. You should get here right away."

Mary's heart sinks. She understands that they would never tell her that either of them had died or that their death was imminent. She also knows from the tone and urgency of the nurse's voice that it's serious, probably involving severe injuries, otherwise they'd let Tracey or Dann talk to her. She wakes Tom and tries to prepare him for the worst, but she can't find the words. "Dann and Tracey were in an accident, and they've been hurt. We need to go to the hospital." She calls her daughter Leslie-Ann, who lives next door, to come and sit with Meghan. Tom and Mary drive to the hospital.

They have been living in Port St. Lucie less than a year and still aren't entirely familiar with the area. Tom knows where Stuart is but not the hospital, so they head in the general direction, following the signs. They can't get there fast enough. Mary is so very worried but still cannot bring herself to tell Tom of her worst fears. She had explained that they were hurt but they would be all right. But in her heart of hearts, she hopes they will get there before . . . She can barely bring herself to consider it. She just wants to see Tracey. Then everything will be okay. It has to be okay.

Mary prays. And prays. Tom doesn't know what to think. *What happened? Was Dann pushing the car a little too hard? Maybe going a little too fast for the road? Did he miss a turn? Why is Mary so quiet, so stoic?* Tom, the eternal optimist, just hopes for the best—that they get to the hospital, maybe find Dann and Tracey a little banged up. *Maybe a short stay in the hospital, out in a few days, get the car fixed—and everything's fine*, he hopes. But nothing prepares them for the scene once inside Martin Memorial Hospital.

Mary and Tom walk nervously into the emergency room. The waiting area is quiet, but Mary peers past the reception desk and sees scores of hospital personnel moving rapidly back and forth. Her heart quickens, the scene all too familiar to her—the organized chaos that comes from being pushed to the edge of panic, saved only by the experience that comes from responding to too many tragedies.

The receptionist directs them into the private room at the back. Mary hates that room—*the room where they tell you what you don't want to hear, the "It's not good" or "There've been very serious injuries" or "It's in God's hands" or worse yet, the "I'm so sorry" room.*

The doctor walks in, takes a deep breath, and tells them the extent of Dann's and Tracey's injuries. "Dann was burned. Badly. But we don't know how extensive yet. Both femurs are broken, and his face appears to have been crushed. We're trying to stabilize him now.

"Tracey wasn't burned, but she's been very seriously injured. She has multiple fractures over her entire body. Her face and lower jaw are broken.

"They both have head injuries, but they're semi-conscious. We don't know the extent of their internal injuries, but we're doing tests now."

"What happened?" Tom asks. Dr. Belle can only shake her head. "They were hit by a drunk driver. It wasn't their fault."

A lifelong teetotaler, Mary cannot believe what she is hearing, but the outrage will have to wait. "Can we see them?" Dr. Belle looks into their eyes, "It's pretty bad. Maybe you should wait until they're stable." But Mary knows better. It might be now or never. Explaining her career as a nurse, she talks her way into the back.

Dr. Belle does her best to prepare them. "You may not recognize them. This isn't going to be easy. You have to be strong."

When Tracey regained consciousness, the first thing she saw was her mom's bright but worried eyes looking back at her. She saw her dad, and felt bad he had to see her like this. It was then that she told her mom she thought she would never see her again. She told them an angel saved her, Jesus took her to heaven, and that she saw Nannie. Tom and Mary didn't know what to make of her words, not sure if she was hallucinating or dreaming, or exactly how real her experience had been. They would find out soon enough.

It is worse than Mary feared. In all her years in the ER back in Wisconsin, the only time she ever saw an accident victim's leg turned almost completely backward was on a patient who later died from her injuries. And now Mary is seeing the very same thing with her own daughter, and worse. Tracey is a bloodied mess, with IV tubes everywhere. Multiple fractures in both femurs, her left ankle crushed, bones protruding. Her right hip broken as well. It is awful. And her face, her beautiful face, is twisted and contorted into a frightful pose. There are open cuts everywhere, and her lower jaw hangs at an odd angle.

Still, Mary looks into Tracey's eyes and sees recognition. Tracey gets out the words, "I thought I'd never see you again."

Mary replies with one of her classic Ohioan idioms, "Just like a bad penny, I'll always show up."

Tom can barely speak. His brain fights against the reality before his eyes—his youngest daughter, a broken shell of herself. *My little girl . . .* He cannot hide his fear and worry. His eyes fill with tears, and all he can say is, "I love you, honey. You'll be fine—we'll take care of Meghan."

After their brief reunion, the medical team rushes Tracey into surgery to begin the massive task of mending her injuries. Her lower jaw is shattered, most of her ribs are broken, as well as her right hip, her pelvis, her knees, her left ankle, and both femurs. As if that weren't enough, Tracey's breathing is labored due to smoke inhalation. A night already far too long grows agonizingly longer as the surgeons take the stage, acting as grand re-weavers as they painstakingly knit together Tracey's broken body.

Tom surveys the room. "Where's Dann?" He grabs Mary's hand and follows a nurse to a curtained area where Dann is supposed to be. They see a figure lying in the bed. "That's not my son-in-law; that's not him," Tom says over and over as he shakes his head. *It can't be, can it?*

Dann's head is twice the normal size, his hair singed and completely burned away on the right side. Blackened skin is peeling from his face, and his eyes are a deep purplish red and bulging. Unaware that he is speaking aloud, Tom continues to cry out, "That is not my son-in-law; that's not Dann!" Mary and the nurses calm him, but still he wonders, *How could anyone live through that?*

The rest of Dann's body is a maze of tubes, blistered skin,

and dressings. But it is Dann. It is the man their daughter loves, the father of their granddaughter, and it doesn't look good. *Is there any way he can survive?* Tom bends down and whispers to Dann through clenched teeth and bitter tears, "You've got to fight, Dann. Tracey and Meghan need you. You've got to fight to live through this. You'll make it. We love you."

It is now after 2 a.m., and Mary knows what she has to do next—call Dann's parents, Jerry and Judy. Though in her job as a nurse she has made calls like this hundreds of times, this time will be different. Nothing could prepare her for this.

Jerry answers and hears Mary's deep, gravelly voice. "Jerry, this is Mary Wills in Florida. Dann and Tracey were in a car accident here and they're in the hospital. They're in critical condition—" then quickly adds, "Meghan wasn't with them, she's fine." All Jerry can get out is "O God, no!"

Mary briefly tells Jerry about Dann and Tracey's injuries, including Dann's extensive burns. A former cop and fireman, he knows from accident scenes the tremendous force it takes to break a femur. He can't begin to grasp the violence it must have taken for each of them to have broken both femurs. This kind of trauma, coupled with burns, made Dann's survival unlikely, if not impossible.

"Mary, tell me how bad it really is."

Relying on her years of nursing experience, she struggles to find the right words. "Jerry, it's bad. I just don't know . . ." Her voice trails off. "Right now they're alive, but they're both hurt very badly. You and Judy need to come as soon as you can, because I don't know how long they can hang on."

After she hangs up, Mary phones the rest of her family to tell them to come to the hospital—Susie, Leslie-Ann, Tommy, and Rob. She needs them here, and knows Tracey and Dann would want to see them too. It is going to be a long night.

In Wisconsin, Jerry and Judy call Dann's brother, Ron, and his sister, Jennifer. Dann's parents make plans to fly to Florida, and by late that morning, they are on their way. Their unspoken fears make their breathing heavy and fill their eyes with tears. Their only hope is to get to Dann and Tracey before it is too late.

3

Head-On Into the Future

Life is a collective series of events, decisions, and circumstances that propel us to where we are at any given moment in time. All of these elements come together to produce a limited set of outcomes, and each of those affects the next. For Tracey and me, our story began in high school.

We were both new students at the school in Germantown, Wisconsin. Tracey had recently moved there from a nearby town, and our family was from southern Illinois. A socially gifted person, Tracey made friends easily and thrived in the structured environment of high school. I struggled against every social norm there was and openly disdained authority. I enjoyed being back in Wisconsin, but I couldn't shake my overall dislike of school. I grew more and more cynical, and for whatever reason—my own insecurities, teenage hormonal surges, uncertain times of the late '70s, or a combination of things—I began to feel a darker and darker world encroaching upon me.

I became more and more angry and rebellious. These attitudes, combined with a growing thirst for living on the edge, led me to the thrills and escapism of marijuana and alcohol. Behavior-wise, Tracey and I could not have been more opposite. We were the same age, both raised in nuclear families with solid Midwestern values—I was Catholic, Tracey was Episcopalian—but that's where anything we had in common ended. Tracey toed the line, while I walked all over it.

However, as my junior year waned, so did my partying, defiant attitude, and constant anger. Inspired by a book my dad gave me, *The Power of Positive Thinking* by Norman Vincent Peale, I turned anew to my faith. It wasn't so much Peale's teaching that I found compelling, but rather that his book led me to search the Bible deeper. I began to see that Christ's words, "I am the way, the truth, and the life," as well as His commands and promises, were intended to give us meaning and direction, particularly me. God no longer seemed to be the distant, harsh patriarch I once imagined. Now I saw Him as my heavenly Father, and in Jesus' parables, such as the prodigal son, I could feel His love. I was on my way to a relationship with Him that brought me peace and joy I had never before experienced.

Reading the Bible again, I remembered another book I had read when I was only thirteen. *Life After Life* by Raymond A. Moody profoundly affected my life. It was full of stories of people who had survived near-death experiences. In my youth, I was deeply intrigued by accounts of angels and heaven. The stories convinced me that the Lord and heaven are very real. Now my new, personal relationship with Christ brought me closer to God.

My previous hunger for God's Word had returned, and by my senior year I had become more at peace with who I was and began to feel more alive and in control of my thoughts and feelings. The cloak of anger, distrust, and bitterness that had darkened my world began to lift.

Even before I began to change my ways, Tracey and I had become unlikely friends. If opposites attract, we had set up a perfect test case. I think we saw each other as something of a challenge. In Tracey, I found the sense of propriety and discipline that I lacked. She sensed in me an adventurous, carefree attitude that she was missing.

By "coincidence," we both chose to attend the University of Wisconsin–La Crosse. I was happy about it for no other reason than pure familiarity, having lived in La Crosse between the ages of five and seven. When we started at La Crosse, Tracey was dating a friend from high school and I wasn't dating anyone. Like any young man, I was looking forward to meeting an entirely new group of girls at college and couldn't wait for her to introduce me to her new friends.

Those first few weeks were a blur—new surroundings, classes, meeting new people, parties, and just plain fun. But with as many girls as I was meeting, I didn't really hit it off with any of them. In retrospect, I guess I was really looking for someone with whom I could have a solid relationship rather than the constant gamesmanship involved with chasing multiple relationships. Still, I was having fun and figured I would eventually meet someone with whom I was compatible.

My first trip back home was in early September for my uncle's wedding. Coincidentally, or perhaps not, Tracey was going to attend the same wedding as the guest of a family friend. We traveled home together and planned to return to school together on Sunday.

The entire wedding was a great celebration, and at one point during the reception, I walked outside for some fresh air. I started down a country road, enjoying the cool night air, and began talking to God. I found myself praying in earnest, asking Him to bring someone special into my life. I was so engrossed in my "conversation" with Him that I must have walked about two miles before returning to the festivities.

The very next day my life changed quite unexpectedly. Tracey and I rode back to La Crosse with other friends, and were sitting in the back seat. At some point our conversation became more serious and personal, and Tracey looked at me and said, "Dann, I think you and I should get to know each other better." I was surprised and asked her what she meant. We were *already* good friends. This time she was even more to the point: "I think we should go out." I was as stunned as I was amused. It simply wasn't something I had considered, and although flattered, I wasn't sure what to make of it. While Tracey and I could talk for hours on almost any subject, and I did think she was a very pretty girl, sometimes it's easy to overlook what's right in front of you. When we arrived in La Crosse, still unsure how to respond, I told Tracey I would call her the next day.

That night as I lay awake in bed, I recalled my words to God about meeting someone special. I asked Him what He had in mind. I had never felt God's hand so clearly, yet I still questioned whether Tracey's comment was His working or just a coincidence.

It was clearly too direct an answer to ignore. It wasn't as if two weeks later I had met someone that I thought I would like and had to work up the nerve to ask out. Tracey had essentially *asked me out* the *next day*. Tracey would later admit that she had no intention of saying that we should "get to know each other better." It was as if the words just sprang from her mouth. Hardly a coincidence!

The following night I stopped by Tracey's dorm room and asked her to take a walk with me. It was the kind of night I really love: The sky was clear, the stars shone brightly, and a dry but cool breeze gently washed over us. The trees seemed to sigh with every small gust, and the dark shadows of the famous La Crosse bluffs loomed in the distance.

We took a meandering walk through the campus and spoke easily about our friendship. Could this—should this—turn into something more? What would happen if it didn't work out? Could we go back to being "just friends"? We had so many questions, yet we knew that neither of us would have any answers unless we took the next step. Tracey said that being together "just felt right," but I still wasn't sure. *Should we just forget about it?*

After walking and talking for well over an hour, we found ourselves nearing her dorm, and with every step I was more conflicted. *Was this what God intended?* We stopped talking, and the silence of the night hung awkwardly in the air. Neither of us wanted to end the evening without making a decision, and doing nothing seemed worse than doing the wrong thing.

It was now or never—my prayers, Tracey's timing of asking me out, the mood of a perfect evening, it was all too compelling to ignore. I turned toward her and pulled her close for a kiss. *Should I really be doing this? Would it mean anything?* All the worries, all the questions, ended when our lips met. There was an unmistakably intense spark, and our hearts and souls melded together. It felt—perfect!

That was September 8, 1980, the first time I knew beyond any doubt that God had intervened directly in my life in response to prayer. And it wasn't more than a week or two later that Tracey and I knew we were in love and even spoke of being married one day. But we had miles to go and a lot of living and growing to do before we got to that point.

As we got to know each other better, I witnessed again and again Tracey's remarkable ability to foresee certain events. She would mention someone that she hadn't seen for some time, and the person would appear within the next few hours, or even minutes, or the phone would ring and they would be calling. Even more remarkable, she would sometimes mention, almost casually, details of significant events that would unfold just days or weeks later. At times, Tracey appeared shaken by the troubling aspects of her visions, but she never really cultivated her ability or dwelled on it too much.

One vivid vision that we had all but forgotten until sometime after our accident, came to her while we were at a party during our freshman year in college. We had been laughing and enjoying ourselves, when without any warning, I found her by herself looking very distressed. "What's wrong?" I asked. Her eyes welled up with tears, and she said, "I just had a vision of us. We were married—and we were killed in a car accident." I didn't know how to respond. Although it was real to her and left her quite distraught, I said, "Oh, come on. You just have an overactive imagination."

That particular vision came to her more than once, though not quite as detailed. She had had prior visions of her own death—at the age of twenty-seven—due to a car accident, but they weren't nearly as vivid or troubling as this one. We never discussed it again, and were only reminded of it after our actual crash years later.

Nevertheless, for the rest of our college days, we seemed to dance away the nights and dream away the days as we chased the future together. Every song was magic, capturing the music of our moods, and speaking only to us. Despite periodic highs and lows, our future together was never in doubt, and on September 7, 1985, just eight months after graduation, we got married.

We quickly settled into the happy and contented roles typical of most newlyweds. Four months previous, Syntex Labs had hired me as a pharmaceutical salesman, and Tracey had found an equally good position with an optical company.

We spent our days working hard and filled our nights and free time with pursuits of fun, fitness, and enjoying life with family and friends.

The only smoke that clouded our bright beginning came on two vacations those first few years together. On a trip in 1986 to Ohio for a Davis family reunion—Mary's side of the family—I shattered my left ankle during a competitive family basketball game. After surgery to place three screws in my ankle, I spent the next few days in the hospital, and with a full leg cast, the trip home was an agonizing venture. I was off work for the next several weeks as my ankle healed. I quickly regained my strength, but my injury put quite a damper on our summer and presaged the problems we would have on a future vacation.

That trip came in 1988, a year that brought a whirlwind of change for us. We began to look for our first house. Tracey's parents were retiring to Florida, and somewhere in between, we were thrilled to discover that Tracey was expecting our first baby, due in December.

Soon after Tom and Mary moved to Port St. Lucie, Florida, we bought a duplex we liked in nearby Jackson (Wisconsin) and would move in early fall. As much as we missed Tom and Mary, our future looked bright and we were as happy as could be.

Before moving, we traveled to St. Thomas, Virgin Islands. As we were eating breakfast one morning, Tracey, about three months pregnant, suddenly had bizarre symptoms where she could not speak and had tingling in her face and arm. Fearing the worst, I thought she was having a stroke, and we found our way to the local hospital. A doctor diagnosed her with an atypical migraine seizure. While painful and very frightening, they are generally not a serious or permanently crippling malady. We breathed a huge sigh of relief but couldn't wait to return home.

Tracey ultimately recovered and we moved into our new duplex just a few months later. We were proud to be in a home of our own, but I knew Tracey still missed having her parents nearby, especially as her due date drew nearer. Her sisters and brothers had moved to Florida years before, and now her entire family was over twelve hundred miles away. At one of the most exciting times of her life, Tracey felt a bit left out, as if she were throwing a party and no one bothered to show up.

By December we had settled comfortably into our new house and had finished all the renovations that truly made it our home. The requisite baby showers and other preparations were finished and we had the baby's room ready for the imminent arrival. On the afternoon of December 13, after sixteen hours of hard labor and a difficult delivery, Meghan came into this world with her big blue eyes drinking in her new world, seeming to study everyone and everything. We couldn't have been more delighted or more contented.

Visiting from Florida, Mary helped with the transition, but with Tracey's long recovery, the hectic time of the holidays, and the steep learning curve that all new parents must navigate, we were exhausted by year's end.

There were a few early bumps on the road to our new normal. Meghan was jaundiced, so it was back to the hospital for tests and treatment. It seemed as though it snowed every other day and it was particularly cold that winter. As typical overcautious first-time parents, other than our trips to the hospital, we would not take Meghan out any more than we had to, so we became a bit housebound. In late January, Tracey also developed severe mastitis and was miserable for several days.

Still missing her parents, exhausted from nightly feedings, and recovering from the delivery, mastitis, and the flu, Tracey sank into a state of complete exhaustion accompanied by feelings she had never before experienced. It was difficult for Tracey to reconcile her expectations of what she felt should be her joy and happiness at being a new mother with the constant exhaustion and inadequacy she now felt. By early March, she was at her lowest point and made an appointment with her doctor.

The doctor explained that hormonal imbalances following pregnancy and delivery followed by her illnesses and sleep deprivation had conspired to send Tracey into a state of post-partum depression. Thankfully, it was quite treatable, and within weeks, the gray cloud of despair that had enveloped her began to dissipate, buoyed by spring's warmer breezes and longer sunny days. She also took a trip to Florida for a short visit with her parents and the rest of her family. She returned with her usual sunny disposition intact, and we were soon making plans for a week-long vacation together in Florida in early September.

This would be our first family vacation together since Meghan's birth. Tracey was eager to spend time with her entire family, and her father in particular was excited to see his new granddaughter. Having had only the brief time with her in March, he looked forward to spending more time with her, especially since she was now almost nine months old and so much more interactive. On September 2, 1989, we were on our way to Florida.

We thoroughly enjoyed ourselves those first few days of the trip. Whether lounging around Tom and Mary's pool, feasting on the various spreads of food, or just laughing and reminiscing with all the family, the entire atmosphere was one of celebration and pure enjoyment. Tracey's struggles were ancient history, Meghan was thriving with all of the attention, and I was as relaxed and happy as could be.

With our fourth anniversary coming on Thursday, Tracey, Tommy, and I agreed to meet in West Palm Beach for dinner. It would give us a chance to meet his girlfriend as well as his friends at the West Palm Beach Police Department, where Tommy was a police officer.

Tracey had not shared her worry and concern about going out that night, and her previous visions had been long forgotten. In spite of her concerns, we were both very much looking forward to our dinner and night out with Tommy.

We left about 6 p.m., gassed up my father-in-law's Ford Merkur, and were on our way. This was the absolute zenith of our lives together. We had each other, a happy, healthy daughter, our own health, great families, great jobs, wonderful friends, and a promising future. Tracey and I spoke many times about how thankful we were for God's many blessings and we felt that life could not get any better for us. In many respects, it never would.

Tracey and me, during our college years

Our wedding,
September 7,
1985

Tracey and Meghan,
July 1989, two months
before the car crash

4

"Did She See Him?"

The next morning, Tracey's father is in the waiting area just outside the ICU, when Pedro Gimenez comes in with a nurse, who directs him toward Tom. With a sense of urgency, he approaches Tom and stands just inches from his face. "Did she see him?" Tom takes a step back. "Who are you? What do you mean?"

Pedro grows more animated. "I was on the highway last night. I was there just after the accident. Did your daughter see the angel?" Tom acknowledges that Tracey had told him and Mary about an angel, but with the confusion in the ER and Tracey's difficulty speaking with her broken jaw and swollen face, he couldn't be sure what to make of it. He

45

listens to Pedro's fascinating recall of the previous night's events.

"I was on the road last night and saw the car burning. I started walking toward the wreck, and there were people running and shouting everywhere. People were screaming that someone was still in the car. It was awful." Pedro continues with tears streaming down his face, "I saw two men run toward the side where your daughter was. One of the men came from the woods! He just glowed, and his eyes were so brilliant, I knew he must be an angel. He appeared out of nowhere. I saw him wipe his hand over her face and tell her that everything was going to be all right . . ." Pedro's voice trails off. "And then he just got up and walked back toward the woods. He disappeared. I couldn't see where he went; he was just—gone!"

Tom looks at Pedro and begins to understand that something more incredible than he could possibly imagine had happened last night. Tracey had haltingly recounted how an angel had helped her and that she had seen her Nannie, Tom's mother-in-law, who had died over twenty-five years ago. She said she saw Jesus, was with an angel, and the angel saved her from dying in the fire.

Suddenly it is much clearer. As agonizing as the previous night had been, as difficult as the waiting is, Tom realizes something incredibly special occurred on the highway last night. *Was it a miracle?* As hard as it is to reconcile the vision of Dann and Tracey's mangled bodies against some kind of divine intervention, something powerful and special had somehow spared them from perishing.

Tom's thoughts race. *How could anyone survive a seventy-mile-per-hour head-on crash? Even the drunk driver was killed, and they always seem to survive. Yet Tracey and Dann are both still alive. Humanly impossible, but with God's grace, maybe they will survive after all.* But still, it seems like too much to hope for so soon. Tom doesn't want to count on their survival when he knows he could hear chilling news at any moment of either of them succumbing to their injuries. Yet the fact that they survived a crash of this magnitude does seem, at least for now, miraculous.

Tom thanks Pedro and says he will tell Tracey about his visit. Pedro says he'll be praying for them.

A lifelong Christian, Tom certainly doesn't doubt God's hand in saving Dann and Tracey, but he has so many questions. *If God sent an angel to save them from death, why not spare them from this suffering as well? Why couldn't He have just prevented the crash?* Tom wants to believe, he wants to know everything will be "all right"—the same words the angel spoke to Tracey. Still, he wants to hear those same words from Tracey. Maybe then he can believe it.

Later that night, Tracey's sister Susie is in Tracey's room when a small knock at the door startles her from an uneasy rest. It is Ben Williams, one of the rescuers, bearing gifts—a Bible each for Tracey and Dann with their names embossed on the cover, a plaque bearing the "Footprints" poem, and a very generous gift of money. Unable to let visitors into the room, Susie and Ben instead leave for a cup of coffee so they can visit.

Susie is overwhelmed by the outpouring of love and concern from complete strangers. When she asks why, Williams tells her, "Last night was an incredible night—and not just the crash and rescue itself." An evangelical Christian who participates in missions around the world, Ben explains that there was so much confusion and activity around the car that he felt all he could do was pray.

Ben prayed desperately and with hopeful expectation for their rescue as he saw his friends first pull Dann from the burning car and then struggle to remove Tracey. Just as Tracey was finally freed from the car, he could not have anticipated the overwhelming power of Christ's healing touch as Tracey was being rescued.

Soon after Ben leaves, the next visitors are Mike Debevec and Kyle Longwell, carrying a beautiful bouquet of flowers for Tracey. As they share more details of the rescue, Susie is touched by their humility. They seem to dismiss their efforts as nothing—as if prying open the door of a burning car to get to Dann and standing on its scorching roof to remove Tracey were somehow ordinary. *Incredible.*

James Vellum stops by a few hours later. He greets Susie with such an intense hug, she nearly loses her breath. He explains what he saw and how he had tried to pry Tracey's door and window open but the board broke. He reiterates what Debevec, Longwell, and the others had previously described and how desperate everyone felt when they could not get Tracey out. Nearly breaking down, Vellum asks, "Did she see him?"

"See who?"

Vellum draws a deep breath and explains, "I saw a man come from the woods just before your sister was pulled out of the burning car." He hesitates before continuing. "I, I . . . I'm telling you, that man was an angel. No one could move her before, but after the angel got there, the other man lifted her out like she was a feather. Then they laid her down on the road, where I was standing. The angel bent over her, wiped his hand across her face, and told her everything would be all right. Then he looked right at me, right into my eyes, almost like he was seeing through me, and just said, 'Take care of Tracey.' That was it. Then he left and walked back into the woods." So moved by the experience, Vellum pulls out a picture he drew of Jesus and asks Susie to give it to Tracey.

I'm still amazed that just minutes after our crash, three men of deep faith—Debevec, Longwell, and Williams—arrived on the scene as others were too panicked and too horrified to act. With Williams fervently praying, Debevec and Longwell moved into action.

I find it beyond coincidence that just as Tracey's life appeared to be lost, three people were praying fervently for her to be saved: Tracey inside the car, a woman on her knees next to the car, and Ben Williams just behind the crowd. And those are the ones we know were praying. I'm certain there were others.

Then several people noticed another man walk onto the scene, and they were convinced he was an angel. Williams felt what he referred to as the "overwhelming healing power of Jesus Christ." As Kyle Longwell reached in to pull Tracey out, he said he felt "a power that just came down on me," and he pulled her free.

This is not fantasy, not wishful thinking, and certainly not coincidence. This was as real as anything in our lives has ever been, or will ever be.

Incredibly, this night would prove to be a prelude to a series of events and situations where God would show us that
no matter what difficulties we might face, He would always
bring blessing in the midst of the trial—and those blessings
would sometimes be as remarkable as the events of this night.

5

The Fight, Round 1

After their plane lands and taxis to the gate at the Fort Lauderdale airport, Jerry and Judy can hardly bear the walk off the plane—not knowing what news awaits them. They spot Tracey's sister-in-law, Vicki Wills—Rob's wife. Vicki is a nurse and can help explain the extent of Dann and Tracey's injuries. But more important, she is there to prepare them for what they are about to see.

They look directly into her eyes, searching for answers. Vicki's returned gaze tells them that, at least for now, Dann and Tracey are still alive. Vicki fills them in as best she can. "You won't recognize Dann. His head and face are very swollen, his eyes are swollen too and purple—they look like plums—and his burns are severe. I just want you to be pre-pared." She lists his other injuries. "Both femurs are broken in several places, he's in traction; almost every bone in his face is broken, his entire right arm and hand is burned, the right side of his face and head are burned, and he has other burns all over his body."

As they arrive at the hospital, Vicki stops them as they get out of the car. "Before you go in, remember—you won't recog-nize Dann. This is going to be hard; I just want to warn you."

They see Tracey first—Dann is just coming out of surgery, and they will have to wait to see him. Tracey is in pelvic trac-tion and leg traction, suspended above her bed with several weights pulling on her bones so they set in proper alignment. She is bandaged from head to toe, her face swollen from the fractures and lacerations. A respirator assists her breathing—her lungs are still stunned from the heat and smoke. As Jerry and Judy reach her side, they struggle for words through their tears. "We love you, Tracey. Keep fighting—Dann and Meghan need you." Tracey can't speak, but her lips form one word—"fire." It is all she can muster.

They leave Tracey's room and reach Dann's. Looking at each other for strength, they take a deep breath and go in. What they see next is beyond anything that Vicki or anyone else could have prepared them for.

The person lying in front of them just couldn't be their son. There is nothing about him they recognize, save for what is left of his black hair. Their legs weaken and their hearts sink. They move forward, holding on to one another for strength. They speak haltingly, struggling to find the right words. "Dann—can you hear us?"

After reminding Tracey to put her seat belt on just before our crash, my next recall came the following day in the hospital. My head had hit the steering wheel and dash so violently that my brain was stunned and shocked into submission. The tiny electrical transmissions that serve to create memory just would not fire—like trying to make a pen write on glass. Whatever consciousness I had could not make its way to my memory. During those first days and ensuing weeks, I seemed to be living in what I perceived to be a very bright white haze, as if I were floating in a brilliant white cloud. When something forced me back to conscious awareness, I felt as if I were pulled back toward physical reality. I have very brief snippets of recall from those first few days that still make me a little sad.

My first full recall was hearing my mom's voice: "Dann, do you know that Meghan wasn't with you in the car? Meghan is fine." My immediate thought was *I can't see anything, I'm lying in a bed, I know I'm in Florida, Mom and Dad are here and they're telling me that Meghan wasn't with us—I must have been in an accident.* My only other thought was *Here it is—the struggle and fight of my life I had always anticipated.* But I wasn't alarmed or worried—I knew I was going to live. I knew I would fight with every ounce of strength possible, but I couldn't tell anyone yet. I couldn't form the words and was too weak to talk.

They tried to reassure me that Tracey was okay—and then, "Dann, do you understand that you've been burned?" Actually, I had no idea, but in that state, it is incredibly difficult to process information beyond what is immediately in front of you. I accepted what I was told—that I had been in some kind of accident in which I had been burned. I didn't question or know the nature or extent of my other injuries. I also accepted my mom's assertion that Tracey was okay.

As they left my room and entered the nearby waiting area, Mom and Dad could barely keep it together. Dad was alarmed by the extent and severity of my injuries. He was particularly upset that my breathing was rapid and shallow—like a dog panting, only faster.

In his years as a cop, fireman, and employee for medical companies, he had never seen anyone as injured as Tracey and I were and still alive. Mom was overwhelmed. To her eyes, it looked nearly hopeless—like my body had been destroyed. She wept with the grief and pain only a mother can feel for her child.

After those initial moments of shock, my parents composed themselves, because they knew they had to keep their emotions in check for both Tracey and me. They felt they needed to fight for us as much as we did.

My next recall has always haunted me. Tracey's Aunt Jane (Mary's sister) from Ohio had flown in and was in my room. I think she was holding my left hand. I was able to open one eye and see what I perceived as the saddest look I have ever seen in anyone's eyes—Aunt Jane looking down at me, telling me she loved me.

Of the first surgeries the doctors at Martin Memorial performed, perhaps the most crucial was the fasciotomy. Severe swelling had stopped blood flow to the muscles and tissues of my right arm, causing a condition known as compartment syndrome. The only way to relieve the pressure was to make a deep incision through the burned flesh, and open the arm from the base of my middle finger to my armpit.

Dr. Juarez told my parents the surgery was only a stopgap measure. To save my arm from amputation, I would need treatment at a burn center. In fact, he told Mom and Dad a burn center was necessary not only to save my arm but my life.

The problem was actually transporting me to a burn center. Dr. Juarez was convinced I needed treatment there, but other doctors told Dad my condition was too grave to survive the helicopter flight.

It was an agonizing decision for my dad. He accepted Dr. Juarez's judgment that Martin Memorial wasn't equipped to handle the severity of my burns. Staying would be a passive choice, almost a death sentence. But an airlift to a burn center was the aggressive choice—if I was going to die, it would only be after a fight. By Sunday morning, September 10, Dad decided I would be moved to a burn center—no matter the risk. The only available bed was at Tampa General, so the plans were set to leave the following day.

At noon on Monday, the medical team prepped me for the flight to Tampa. Loaded with IVs, monitors, wrapped in bulky dressings, and wearing special traction pants, they wheeled me down the hallway. With both families in tow, we had one stop to make before I went out to the heliport: Tracey's ICU room so we could say good-bye to each other.

It is amazing how our brains worked to protect us while we were in that state. Tracey and I both recall seeing each other as completely normal—doing our best to talk through our swollen, broken faces and clenched jaws. I don't know if I actually saw her or just thought I did.

I remember our words to each other. I said, "I love you, honey. Stay strong, keep fighting—I love you." Tracey replied,

"I love you, too—just get better and we'll be together soon." I'm sure those around us did not share our optimism—there was not a dry eye among our escorts. For each of us to have survived the initial impact required angelic intervention; for both of us to survive the odyssey that awaited us can be explained only by further divine guidance.

The unspoken fear that Tracey and I would never see each other again accompanied me to the heliport. Since my dad was the one that authorized the life-flight to Tampa, his heart was particularly heavy. As he stared at the departing helicopter growing distant against the vast Florida sky, his heart went with me—almost certain he would never see me again.

Thankfully, the flight to Tampa was uneventful. I briefly recall feeling warm ocean breezes swirling around me after we landed and the doors of the helicopter were opened. Unfortunately, my first memory inside the hospital was that of a male nurse cursing loudly and shouting, "We don't have a bed for him!"

Because I wasn't able to think clearly, much less respond, I thought I had been abandoned. I believed I was lying in a hallway in the hospital. I couldn't see and had no idea where I was. The most vivid memories from the remainder of that day and night were of pure pain. It was like ten thousand pounds of agony piercing every cell in my body—each screaming out to me in torment. It was everywhere and nowhere. I would try to concentrate on one small site of pain, try hard to control it, capture it, make it go away, and then I was hit by another wave from my leg, my arm, my head, or my face.

It was relentless, until I felt as if I didn't have a body anymore, just a vessel of pain. I became the pain. As it washed over me again and again, my brain seemed to shut down and I fled once more into the white light. I never really felt like I was dying, it was more like an altered state of reality, neither conscious nor unconscious, not quite dead but not fully alive—hovering between the two.

As I lay in agony that day, time had no bearing on my reality. The nurse's dismissive comments and my intermittent states of consciousness had me believing I remained in the hallway for several days.

What I did not know was that somewhere between loading me on the helicopter and arriving in the ER at Tampa, my chart had been lost. The doctors at Tampa had no way of knowing what meds I had or had not been given and no history of my injuries or condition that either required or contraindicated any additional medications—so I was without any pain meds for almost the entire day and into the night.

I still don't know why a fax or phone call to Martin wouldn't have been sufficient, but I had to undergo an entire battery of fresh tests and procedures for the Tampa staff to determine my status. I felt like a piñata that had been beaten with baseball bats and set on fire, then tossed aside to wallow in the agony of my wounds.

I don't know when I finally got morphine again, but the last thing I remember of that hellish day was writhing through another scan. I wouldn't be fully cognizant and aware until almost three weeks later.

Tracey's first days and weeks were all too clear for her. After enduring the previous night's agony in the ER, she woke up after the surgeries to repair her jaw, hip, and ankle to a new form of torture—suspended above a hospital bed in pelvic and leg traction, with her left leg in a cast to further support the metal holding her crushed ankle in place.

Consumed by pain, Tracey winced with every breath and screamed in silence with every twitch of her battered muscles. She was so beaten, bruised, and broken by her injuries and so bound up with traction wires and cables that her body was unable to respond to the demands of her brain.

Incredibly, even in the midst of severe pain, Tracey frequently awoke with a song in her heart and on her lips: "Holy, Holy, Holy! Lord God Almighty!" or "Hosanna, Hosanna, Hosanna, Blessed Is He Who Comes in the Name of the Lord." Clearly Tracey had been in the presence of Jesus, nearly saw the face of God, and been touched by an angel. I believe when Tracey "died," somewhere in the background of her experience, she either heard this music and it seeped into her soul or she was so moved at being in the Lord's presence that these songs of praise sprung from her soul spontaneously and she sang along—praising the Lord for the blessings and miracles He had brought to us.

In contrast to the celestial songs of praise that brought Tracey so much peace, the cacophonic sounds of the crash were buried deep within her—screeching tires, breaking glass, grinding metal, and our own screams invaded her sleep and thrust her into the horror afresh.

Tracey spent her days dreading the nights—as dusk descended her anxiety increased. The silence of the hospital at night magnified everything. A glass crashing to the floor became our car crash—every sound forced her to relive the horror over and over.

The other battle that Tracey continued to fight in her first days and weeks in the hospital, along with her physical struggle to survive, was a spiritual fight. The crash that caused such complete devastation of her life was so unexpected and so out of the realm of anything she had ever experienced or conceived that she could not reconcile her new reality against what was once the promise of her future. That conflict manifested itself in a deep rage—against the drunk driver, against the reality of her condition, even rage at herself for feeling the way she did. She knew she had had a divine experience, but she also knew it had come at a steep price.

Other struggles fueled Tracey's anger and fear, especially hearing from her orthopedic physician that she may never walk again. This weighed heavily on her mind. The athleticism of her youth was gone—her dreams of running after Meghan and having more children seemed over.

Her one hope rested with a surgery to place rods in each femur. But the night before the procedure, Tracey developed a sudden shortness of breath and a very high fever with confusion and other neurological symptoms. Fatty emboli, which can develop when the long bones of the legs are broken and marrow leaks into the bloodstream, were clogging capillaries and blood vessels. The emboli forced her doctor to cancel the surgery—ending her hopes of escaping traction and taking away her best chance of walking again.

Still other challenges surfaced. Not long after the fatty emboli incident, Tracey developed a clot in her left calf, just above her shattered ankle. Though her surgeon had repaired her ankle as best he could with screws and plates, she still needed a cast to keep all the shattered pieces in place. With the immobility of pelvic and leg traction and almost no movement to keep her leg muscles pumping, her pooling blood eventually clotted and painfully swelled her calf. She faced the possibility that a clot could form and threaten her leg, or worse, break free and cause death. Once again, however, with proper treatment and perhaps divine intervention, Tracey's body defeated another threat to life and limb.

Amid her physical and spiritual battles, Tracey fought a third adversary—doubt. Despite assurances from her family and visitors, until she could see me for herself, or at least hear my voice, she didn't trust that I was alive. Her last vision of me, other than our brief good-bye prior to my flight to Tampa, was of my body being pulled, on fire, through the window of our car. She couldn't erase that vision from her mind and would ask nearly everyone, "How's Dann?" Susie recalls that Tracey would ask her to come near to her bed and stare into her eyes and ask again and again, "How's Dann?" searching deep into Susie's eyes for any hint that she might be lying about my true status.

One night Tracey seemed particularly weak. Her mother had become more concerned about her sagging spirits, and after Tracey again asked about me, Mary firmly responded, "Look, you need to concentrate on yourself. *Dann is alive—* you're going to have to accept that. I promise I'll tell you if anything changes. Right now, you have to realize that this is a battle, and you're never going to see him or Meghan again if you don't concentrate on your getting well." Mary's stern words seemed to be enough to calm Tracey's fears. She knew her mom well enough to know she was right.

Other anxieties came in waves. Despite the horrors through which she had already lived, the one thing that upset her most was being told she might not be able to bear more children. Tracey's preferred identity in life was that of *Mom*. Regardless of her other accomplishments, the one thing she treasured most was being a mother. Though we had Meghan, we had talked of having more children.

Another fight that continued to sap Tracey's strength was the issue of forgiveness. She seethed with anger at the drunk driver who hit us. *How could he be so careless, so completely irresponsible, so self-absorbed in his own sick dependencies?* She knew at some point she would have to forgive him so that she could heal, but her constant pain made forgiveness close to an impossible task. She worried that she would die before she found a way to forgive him. She didn't want to face God without having forgiven him.

In the end, the conflicting feelings of rage and peace helped Tracey heal. She drew from her anger the energy to fight, and in the peace drawn from the Holy Spirit, the forbearance necessary to endure the fight for her life.

"Fighting for your life" is an overused, underappreciated, and misunderstood phrase. It is much more than a determination to stay alive. It describes what it takes to survive a desperate situation in which you are clinging to life while death has you in its cold grip. It is as real a decision and as active a physical and mental process as anything one will ever do in life.

In our dire circumstance, it felt as though our entire universe—its loves, joys, sorrows, memories, hopes, and dreams—were compressed into a small ember glowing deep within our souls. It took everything we had to keep that spark alive. It took our will to live and God's grace and strength to carry us through our ordeal from the first instant of the crash and through those first few weeks.

After I arrived at Tampa General, the real work for me began. Despite the rough start on my first day there, my care was actually quite impressive. Burn specialist plastic surgeons, trauma surgeons, orthopedic surgeons, cardiologists, internists, and a psychiatrist made up the treatment team that would effect and manage my restoration.

My mom and dad would also stay with me throughout my hospitalization in Tampa to oversee my care. I was incapable of making even basic decisions, and with Tracey two hundred miles away, incapacitated by her own injuries, there was no other alternative.

The orthopedic physicians explained their initial plans to my parents. They would repair my shattered femurs with inserted rods, allowing for quicker healing and giving me some ability to move in bed without being trapped in traction, also reducing the risk of pneumonia. Just as important, having rods in the femurs would eliminate the risk for possible infection from the traction pins.

When my dad questioned the necessity of this surgery, both surgeons responded with the same emphasis: "This is his ONLY chance at survival." Virtually every burn patient eventually develops some infection, but by placing the rods, the doctors hoped to limit the likelihood of a deadly infection.

After two days of stabilization in the ICU burn unit, my first surgery at Tampa was the most extensive—excision of my burns and grafting. Like many surgeries, the details can seem brutal but are necessary for a successful outcome. As burned and damaged skin is scraped away and removed, it is cut down to bleeding tissue. Healthy tissue is harvested with a dermatome—an instrument similar to a potato peeler that excises healthy skin in approximately four-inch-wide strips. The surgeon then perforates the donor skin to help it expand, so a single strip of donor skin can stretch to cover an area several times larger than its original size.

The grafts were laid in a quilt-like pattern, stapled into place, and wrapped with non-adherent gauze. The donor sites were covered with a biosynthetic skin substitute that adhered to the tissue underneath as it healed.

My only memory of that day is being wheeled from surgery to recovery and hearing a nurse or technician say to someone else, "Wow, he's really sucking up the blood. This is the nineteenth unit we've hung." This didn't cause me any alarm—I was still in that mode of acceptance without really thinking anything through. I had lost almost twice the normal blood volume in one surgery. In fact, I had thirty units of blood, platelets, and plasma during that surgery.

The next surgeries were performed in the following two days, when the rods were inserted into each femur. By this point, the number of units of blood I received surpassed fifty, and my dad stopped counting. This was 1989, when AIDS, hepatitis C, and other blood-borne pathogens were still poorly understood, a fact that would come back to haunt me years later.

On September 21, two weeks after the crash, another outstanding plastic surgeon, Dr. Karen Walsh, repaired the fractured bones in my face. Initially prepared to place four to six plates to bring the bones back into alignment, she quickly determined that the CT scans weren't as accurate as hoped.

With several fractures across my face and my sinuses essentially crushed, she could find only one solid bone—on the left side of my face—and she affixed a single plate. It was the best she could do, manually moving the rest of my bones back into place to get the best possible anatomical alignment. Since my lower jaw was unbroken, Dr. Walsh used it as a solid platform to help stabilize my upper facial bones and then wired my jaw shut. With her extensive work, I had a decent outcome. However, due to the massive trauma, I still suffer chronic sinus infections and pain.

Most of my memories from those first three weeks in the hospital were brief snippets. I can remember some visits with Mom and Dad and my brother and sister, but I can't remember much else that was meaningful.

I do remember thinking that my sister Jenn's wedding was approaching. She and John were to be married on September 30, and it hurt me to know that Tracey and I would miss it. In addition, I knew that on a day that should be full of happiness and celebration, many of their thoughts would be with us.

As Jenn's wedding drew closer, I began to emerge from the fog that had clouded my thoughts and obscured my memory. I was almost three weeks from the severe concussion and a full week past my last surgery. Nonetheless, I was still having trouble distinguishing fantasy from reality. Hallucinations and dreams melded with actual thoughts and information, becoming my reality—part fiction, part truth. And one of these created thoughts ran through my mind over and over again.

I knew a drunk driver had hit us, but I was not aware of the exact details and circumstances. I had a recurring dream or hallucination that Tracey and I were on a two-lane highway. I was driving too fast for the road, and as I swept through a curve underneath a bridge, I wandered over the center line and struggled to correct my speed and maintain control of the car. Just then a young driver, who had had a little too much to drink, lost control of his car and also crossed the center line—hitting us head on.

Although this scenario was pure fantasy, as far as I was concerned it was my reality, and it continued to play out in my mind. I experienced terrible feelings of guilt. I had assumed the driver was a young man who made a mistake and paid for it with his life.

But what really tore me apart night and day, even as my thoughts became more lucid, was that I had hurt Tracey. I had failed to protect my wife, the mother of my daughter. Even though I knew a drunk driver had contributed to the accident, I felt that I should have been able to avoid it—that I was as responsible for Tracey's injuries as anyone.

Just the week before our tragedy, I had avoided a driver who came at me the wrong way over a hill. *Why couldn't I have prevented this?* As I lay in my hospital bed, the guilt was killing me. I was struggling to live while my heart was dying.

Mom and Dad were increasingly concerned about leaving me while they attended the wedding. Though it had been three weeks, my survival was not yet certain. Dad noticed I had become increasingly listless and my spirits were sagging—he thought I was losing my will to live.

The night before leaving for Wisconsin, Dad tried to re-assure me that he and Mom would only be gone a few days and that Tracey's family would stay with me in their absence. My mind, still somewhat muddled and hazy, was heavy with thoughts of Tracey. I looked up at Dad from my bed with a vacant gaze and asked, "What are they going to do to me?" He just looked at me quizzically. "What do you mean?" My voice quiet and distant, I answered, "I hurt Tracey. I don't know what they're going to do to me."

Not an overtly emotional man, Dad looked like a tidal wave of hurt had just washed over him and tears came to his eyes. In retrospect, his heart was breaking at the realization that I didn't know the exact circumstances of our crash. "Dann, don't you know what happened?" I didn't want to hear it. In my mind, I knew what I had done—my carelessness had caused Tracey's pain. I shook my head and closed my eyes, thinking, *Please don't tell me.* I did not want to hear aloud what I had done.

Dad grabbed my shoulders. "Dann—look at me. You have to hear this."

"No, no!" I replied, still shaking my head, tears filling my eyes.

"Dann, it wasn't your fault. You were driving on a six-lane divided freeway—you were hit by a drunk driver who was going the *wrong way*." Staring into my eyes for emphasis, he continued, "Dann, he was driving on the wrong side of the freeway. You weren't doing anything wrong—there was a car in front of you that swerved at the last second. There was nothing you could have done. The man who hit you had a blood-alcohol level of over .28—he was completely wasted.

It was at least the fourth time he had been driving drunk—he had three other DWIs. Dann, it was *not* your fault."

Dad held on to me, and I cried, waves of relief washing over me. I still felt guilty that I couldn't have somehow prevented this agony, but now I finally understood—it was not my fault. There was no two-lane highway where I had drifted over the center line, no bridge, no curved road. This wasn't a careless mistake by a young driver with just a little too much to drink.

Though I now knew the details of the accident, I could not bring myself to be angry or to hate the driver for his indifference to the eventual outcome of his negligence. I could not see any benefit to my holding any animosity against him. It would only hinder my recovery.

As Tracey struggled through her feelings, she eventually came to the realization that if the man could have known the pain and destruction he had wrought he would have been horrified and full of remorse. But ultimately, Tracey knew that her forgiveness was not dependent upon someone else's remorse, real or imagined. Her forgiveness must come from deep within herself. Christ's words "Father, forgive them" seeped into her soul, and God's love and peace drove out the bitterness and anger she had been harboring. Her journey toward forgiveness had begun.

Neither Tracey nor I had any wish, then or now, that the other driver suffer penalty for his error. It is not our call, and we trust in God's compassion. Forgiveness is not an easy task. In fact, it is not a singular task, but a practice. Jesus said we must forgive "seventy times seven," which means it is an ongoing process.

Forgiveness benefits the giver more than the offender. Harboring a grudge does nothing to the perpetrator of a misdeed. Hatred is a sweet poison that may be satisfying at first taste, but once swallowed, seeps deep within to eat away at the soul, leaving a bitterness that taints everything in life.

As we began our fourth week in the hospital, even though infection and other threats persisted, it was becoming more and more evident that both Tracey and I would survive. While still fighting with every ounce of our strength, we had surrendered control of our recovery to God.

Tracey's other inspiration was Meghan. As early as the first week, someone in the family, usually her father, would drive Meghan to the hospital and take her into Tracey's room. As agonizing as it was for Tracey to see Meghan without being able to hold her, the mere sight of her was a powerful incentive for Tracey to return to being "Mom" as soon as she could.

Because my awareness was still diminished throughout those first few weeks, my only thoughts about Meghan were a general sense of sadness that I couldn't be with her. I knew she was in good hands, and everyone made a point of telling me that she was doing well and asking for "Da-Da" quite a bit. I had resolved early on to heal as quickly as possible and return to both Meghan and Tracey.

6

Tom's Mission

"Operation: Meghan"

Of the many blessings that resulted from the crash, one true gift was the strong bond forged between Tom and Meghan. It developed into an iconic image of the doting, protective grandfather and the happy, babbling baby.

Together they were a ray of hope and light, especially in those first few weeks when our lives were hanging in the balance. However, for Tom, his relationship with Meghan was more than a genuine love and affection for his grand-daughter—it was a responsibility that Tom took seriously, and I've only recently come to understand what an immense task this must have been for him.

Tom saw himself as responsible not only for Meghan's day-to-day care, but in his eyes he was single-handedly responsible for seeing that Meghan came out of this experience safe, healthy, and without any emotional trauma. Perhaps even more important, he knew that Meghan was vital to keeping both Tracey and me motivated not only to survive our ordeal but to live as fully and capably as possible.

From the moment Tom and Mary heard Tracey recount the details of her near-death experience, it was clear to them that Tracey returned to her earthly life for one reason—Meghan. She had assumed I was already dead. She came back because she didn't want Meghan to live without both parents—and that fact certainly didn't escape Tom.

Tom was close to all of his children, but Tracey was his youngest daughter—his baby—and he wouldn't disappoint her.

While Tracey and I were still in school at La Crosse, I noticed their bond from the instant I first met Tom. Tracey's eyes lit up when he entered the room, and that never changed. Tom and I hit it off immediately. It was easy to understand Tracey's love and respect for her father. He was a gifted conversationalist, had a great sense of humor, and had a way of putting everyone at ease. In many ways—from the incredible stories of his youth, his Navy days during WWII, and in the span of time that I knew him—he reminded me of a modern-day Tom Sawyer. I had enormous respect for him. As a husband, father, grandfather, father-in-law, and Christian—he was the real deal. The fact that he took so seriously the job of becoming Meghan's chief guardian, protector, and foster parent was not surprising to any of us.

Upon returning home the day after the crash, he practically snatched Meghan away from Tracey's sister, Leslie-Ann, who had been watching her. Gathering Meghan in his arms, he announced to Mary, "I won't be of much use at the hospital. You're going to have to stay with Tracey to make sure she gets the care she needs. I'll take care of Meghan." From that point forward it seemed that Tom's training and discipline from his navy days returned to him and his mission-ready sense of duty surged. Meghan was his ship, and he was sentry, crew, and captain.

Grandpa Tom and Meghan, February 1990

Tom's devotion to Meghan was also the best outlet he had in the midst of the crisis atmosphere that had descended upon our world. Meghan became Tom's substitute for us; she was a piece of us, a vital connection to our lives, and the most significant way he could help—even participate in—our recovery. Through his loving care of Meghan, he was reaching out to us and pouring his love *through* her to us.

He not only dedicated himself to Meghan's care, he studied her and almost came to know her as a mother knows her child. He could read her moods and needs nearly before she felt them herself. There were many visitors in those days, especially early on, and he noticed how Meghan would suddenly turn toward every new voice, staring intently, as if to ask, "Mom, Dad—is that you?" It nearly broke his heart, but he made sure that she wanted for nothing else. She almost never cried because Tom fed her just before she became too hungry, changed her before she became uncomfortable, and put her down for a nap or bedtime before she became too tired.

In her first eight months, Tracey had Meghan on a routine schedule of feedings, naps, playtime, and bedtime. Tom took that schedule to an entirely new level of regimentation. With the *USS Meghan,* he ran a tight "ship" and adhered to an exact schedule. It became well known among the family that if anyone wanted to take Meghan out to the park or lunch or to see Tracey, they had to get permission from Tom first—and they had better make sure Meghan got her feedings and naps at the scheduled times.

Tracey's brother Rob and his wife, Vicki, experienced this firsthand one afternoon when they took Meghan out for a while to give Tom a break—not that he wanted it. They had a completely different understanding of "out for a while" than did Tom. For Tom, it meant an hour or two—tops. For Rob and Vicki, it quite innocently meant "We're going out, and we'll be back when we get back."

They left in late morning. Tom's pacing started about 1 p.m. He called their home, twice—leaving messages on their answering machine. He called Tommy, then Leslie-Ann, and then paged Mary at the hospital and repeatedly walked back and forth from the house to the driveway. He was desperate for a sighting, as if his ship had sailed without him and he could not safely defend her from threats that seemed everywhere. Tom was worried and more than a little annoyed.

Finally he spotted them as they drove up the street several hours later. He met them in the driveway, not the least bit reassured by their smiles and Meghan's bright eyes—this called for an inspection. Barely pausing for a breath between questions, much less an answer, he machine-gunned queries at them. "Did you feed her? What did she eat? Has she had a bottle? Where were you? Did she nap? Has she been changed?" Tom hadn't shown much emotion throughout our ordeal, but it all came pouring out now through his concern for Meghan, She was *his* charge, *his* responsibility—she had been a ship over the horizon and now she was safely back in port—never to leave without him again; he just couldn't risk it.

He was not a mere caretaker of his precious granddaughter, it was as if he were the keeper of the holy grail, the very reason we would survive and live life once more. And he would do everything within his power and ability to keep her safe for our return. But it wasn't just about us; he saw to it that Meghan provided a needed distraction for everyone. She was the ray of hope and brightness that only one so young and innocent can provide in such darkness.

Tom documented Meghan's every accomplishment, whether mundane or monumental. The video camera was always nearby, ready for those fleeting moments that he judged too precious to miss. He didn't want us to miss out on any more of Meghan's life than he knew we must. I also think that deep inside he wanted documented proof of his good care, as much for our reassurance as for his own memories. The evidence was overwhelming—the hours of footage he took were every bit as precious as he had hoped. Meghan was clearly healthy, happy, and thriving under his care.

Nothing escaped his eyes and nothing was too good for Meghan. Returning one afternoon after visiting Tracey in the hospital while Leslie-Ann watched Meghan, he picked her up and, looking at Leslie-Ann, said, "Her diaper is wet, have you changed her?" Rolling her eyes a bit, Leslie-Ann replied, "Dad, she just had a bottle." Then she added, "Diapers aren't meant to stay dry. There's a reason we use them—she's fine!"

It wasn't just family that felt the heat of Tom's hawklike protection; anyone in Meghan's immediate vicinity was subjected to the protective cocoon Tom had wrapped around her. Our best friends from Wisconsin, Andy and Wendy, traveled to Florida to see Tracey in late October. Wendy and Tracey were childhood friends and quite close. One night during their stay they had stopped to see Meghan and visit with Tom near dinnertime. Meghan was already sitting in her high chair, and Wendy began feeding her some baby food. Hovering nearby, Tom suddenly reached out and grabbed the spoon from Wendy. "You're not feeding her right; I'll take over." Wendy was surprised but also amused—by now, Tom's watchful care had become legendary. He meant no harm or insult—he wasn't that kind of person—but in his eyes, he alone was capable of Meghan's proper care.

Tom did a wonderful job with Meghan and forged a beautiful bond—she thrived under his doting and was completely happy and healthy the entire time Tracey and I were hospitalized.

Mission accomplished!

7

The Fight, Round 2

"The Awakening"

By the end of September, Tracey and I had both turned the corner from a moment-by-moment fight for survival to a more settled hour-by-hour and day-to-day approach. I was emerging from the fog that had clouded my thoughts and obscured my memory. The last hallucinations seemed to subside and I was more lucid. Tracey's delusions and anxieties had diminished as well.

With most of our surgeries behind us, we settled into our separate routines. Various family members filled Tracey's days with visits. Tracey's mom would stay most nights— her nursing background a tremendous comfort. Desperately struggling to get some kind of control back in her life, with Mary nearby, Tracey felt she could let her guard down and relax. After Mary would spend the night, Tom or another family member would relieve her and spend the day with Tracey, everyone doing their best to keep her company, sometimes taking Meghan along for visits as well.

Sometime after her third week in the hospital, Tracey was taken out of pelvic traction, which allowed her to lie more fully in her bed. However, as she found more comfort, she also found her days to be sheer monotony—waiting for her shattered bones to repair themselves.

Tracey drew her strength from the Holy Spirit. With her early anger dissipated, she concentrated on the love and peace that remained with her from her near-death experience. It had been so completely filled with the love of God, the healing touch of Jesus, and the peace of the Holy Spirit, that she felt compelled to share it with virtually every visitor, nurse and doctor, almost anyone who walked through her door. People couldn't help but be drawn in, filled with the wonder of her experience. She made sure everyone knew that her journey to heaven happened for one reason alone—her faith in the risen Christ, who suffered for our sins.

A frequent visitor was the hospital chaplain. Pastor Blanchard had intended to build Tracey's faith and help her understand God's purposes in the midst of such a traumatic and painful ordeal. But her dynamic, unshakable faith gradually turned the tables on the pastor, who found himself listening more than counseling. Toward the end of her hospital stay, he stopped in one afternoon to visit. "I need to tell you something, Tracey." He hesitated, and with eyes glistening, continued, "Before we met, I was struggling with some very profound doubts. I want you to know"—his voice now cracking—"that your strength and your faith have helped restore my own faith. I can't thank you enough." Tracey marveled at the ways in which God used their routine visits to minister to both of them.

My days were also filled with routine—a mixture of pain, anxiety, fear, dread . . . and relief. There were the vital-sign checks, as well as the daily dressing changes of the grafts, donor sites, and burns.

I would wake up sweaty from the previous night, pain emanating from any one of the wounds on my body, and knew that I would have to submit to the usual rounds of attending physicians, followed by the team of nurses that came to do the dressing changes. I looked forward to the IV drip of morphine a few minutes before this, and knew that for at least a few hours afterward, no one would bother me.

I must say that the nurses were outstanding, and I marvel to this day at the dedication, courage, and compassion burn nurses must have to accomplish their daily tasks. They are remarkable people and care for their patients with an uncommon devotion.

My chest was covered with a biosynthetic overlay (artificial skin) that allowed the donor sites to heal. These sites were generally more painful even than the burned areas. The overlay hardened to a solid mass and cracked with my every movement. It acted as a large scab that was peeled away as the skin beneath it regenerated. It was a necessary process, but quite painful.

The other issue I had to deal with was the overall appearance of my body. My naturally dark skin that tanned easily was now a mass of scar tissue. The graft sites were a maze of pebbled flesh, and the donor sites were mostly raw, leaving areas robbed of pigmentation. The fingertips of my right hand were blackened char and came to a shriveled point.

It would be some time before I could look in a mirror. The entire right side of my face had been burned. But since the skin on the face has a remarkable ability to regenerate, Dr. Crenshaw wanted to see if this area would recover without grafting. The surface of my right ear had burned away, but since the back of the ear was intact, my doctors hoped it would repair itself as well.

At the end of the daily routines, the nurses would carefully massage lotion onto the healing areas to maintain their moisture and elasticity. Then they would change the bedding and wrap me in fresh dressings and gauze; with the wraps in place the pain would subside. I would actually feel refreshed—and exhausted.

Exhaustion was a constant companion for both of us. Having endured our extensive traumas and surgeries, our bodies consumed themselves from within to get the energy needed to repair tissue and bone. We both lost a significant amount of weight; I went from 175 pounds to less than 130 and Tracey from 120 to about 80 pounds.

My parents returned just a few days after my sister's wedding, and soon afterward I was upgraded from the burn ICU to the burn floor. From that point on, I regained most of my conscious awareness and ability to recall daily events.

On October 5, I had another surgery for more skin grafting to repair some areas that hadn't healed. The primary reason for this surgery, however, was to amputate the burned fingertips on my right hand. I was actually relieved that I no longer had to look at the charred remains.

Dr. Crenshaw also placed K-wires through the remaining joints in my fingers to prevent them from bending and flexing, allowing the grafts to heal. The long, thin wires that extended from each joint were topped by a pearl-like ball, keeping my hand in a fixed position.

With renewed awareness, I missed Tracey terribly. Mom and Dad had told me the extent of her injuries, but it was still difficult to comprehend. They reassured me that she was healing, but I wanted to see her, touch her, take care of her, and let her know that everything was going to be all right.

Sometime around the fourth week in the hospital, we were able to speak briefly on the phone. What joy and relief it was to hear her voice, but I don't think we made it more than a few seconds without weeping. From that point on, we were able to talk a couple of times each week. I was always in a better mood after hearing Tracey's voice.

It was about this time that I became more aware of Tracey's near-death experience. I had always felt that Tracey had a special faith, and to know that God had directly intervened in our lives to return her to Meghan and me enhanced my own faith and made me feel that both Tracey and I were left on earth to fulfill a more meaningful destiny. I began telling everyone I could about our story, especially Tracey's visit with Jesus and angelic encounters. Most were as enthralled as I was.

It is impossible to ignore the many extraordinary circumstances and events that had to come together for both Tracey and me to live through a seventy-mile-an-hour head-on crash.

Typically, a crash like ours is not survivable—especially without air bags.

From the moment of the accident, when rescuers and bystanders knelt to ask God to save us from almost certain death, to our months in the hospital, the fervent prayers of God's people were offered up and countless blessings returned to us. Tracey and I were blessed with a network of support that leads me to marvel at God's love. This love even came through complete strangers who, having read or heard of our plight, visited, phoned, or sent cards, offering their prayers and well-wishes. It was truly overwhelming. I believe the prayers of God's faithful made the difference between life and death, disability and healing.

The doctors and nurses who cared for us were further examples of God's love. Their care, concern, and reassurance were vital to our recovery. We each came to favor a particular nurse who seemed to best ease our worries and concerns. Tracey's special nurse was Jane, who was able to move Tracey in such an effortless and reassuring manner that she provided her with the confidence and trust she so desperately craved. Where Tracey once dreaded every move and procedure, she now found peace and comfort under Jane's care.

My own special nurse was Carol, a slender brunette who moved with the effortless grace of a dancer and brought an air of tranquility with her every time she breezed into my room. Her melodic voice was music to my ears and soothed my anxious heart. I first met Carol after I was moved to the burn floor from ICU, and from our very first interaction, I felt I was in the presence of someone special, very kind and caring.

I have often thought about the many special people we met as a result of our tragedy, and believe it is one of the ways God brings blessing out of such circumstances. The support we had was crucial as we endured the many ups and downs throughout our hospitalization. Tracey and I went from a happy, healthy, vibrant family to a shattered dream in an instant. The fear and uncertainty of being able to reclaim our once idyllic life while we fought first to survive, and then to heal were more than either of us could have possibly endured alone.

I thank God we had our parents to watch over us, care for us, and simply offer encouragement. Though Tracey and I were adults with a child of our own, there is no substitute for the love of a parent. I knew our parents loved us as much as we loved Meghan.

I missed Meghan terribly throughout my hospital stay; thinking about her was a constant source of both inspiration and frustration. I knew she was safe and happy, but it hurt knowing I was missing her first steps and words. I loved being a dad and wanted to enjoy every minute of Meghan's life. As I would gaze at the portrait of her that hung in my hospital room, I vowed to return to her as soon, and as completely, as I could.

I would have liked someone to take Meghan to Tampa to visit me but it just wasn't practical. Even if that could have been arranged, my doctors would not have allowed the risk of Meghan's possibly exposing me to dangerous bacteria, or for that matter, my exposing her to germs. I had already tested positive for Methicillin-Resistant Staph Aureus (MRSA) and was in isolation for my entire stay. MRSA is a nasty bacterium—if it spreads and becomes an active infection it is difficult to treat and quite deadly, especially for patients with other medical problems.

One of the miracles of my recovery was the fact that I never developed any kind of infection. When I entered Tampa General, I had several strikes against me—with burns on greater than 30 percent of the body, the risk of infection increases dramatically, and the MRSA, fractures, surgeries, intravenous tubes, catheter, feeding tube, and long hospital stay all increased my risk as well.

The doctors had told my parents it was just a matter of time before I would get an infection—not *if* but *when*. However, I had several factors working in my favor—excellent medical care, the hawklike protection of my parents, who made certain that every visitor paid strict attention to the sterile precautions in my room, and of course the hundreds of prayers.

8

The Fight, Round 3

As our miracles mounted, Tracey and I continued to heal and progress toward our ultimate goal of reuniting. By the middle of October, we knew our hospital stay would be ending at some point, but our next steps were filled with uncertainty. We truly had no concept of the struggles that awaited us. We were both blissfully ignorant of our true conditions and had no idea of the extraordinarily long road of rehab and recovery that lay before us.

Tracey still could not walk, and there was considerable doubt that she would ever walk without assistance. I was going to need additional therapy to regain the use of my right hand, which was stiff and rigid from the burns and surgeries and completely useless. We were both physically weak from our extended stay in hospitals, and it would take months to rebuild our stamina and strength to the point where we could function independently. We also needed additional surgeries. And while it was apparent that we would need to stay in Florida and near our doctors for the continuity of our care, exactly where that would be—and if we could be together—had yet to be decided.

The last few weeks of our acute care prepped us for our eventual discharge and release to a rehab hospital. We had several milestones to meet before that could happen. We had scans and tests to determine if our bones had healed enough to bear our weight, and in the biggest step yet, Tracey's leg traction was to be removed, an event she eagerly anticipated. A hostage to her bed throughout her stay, the thought of breaking free from the traction pins and weights was almost more than she could bear.

Many questions loomed: How completely would we recover? Would we walk normally again? Would I regain the use of my right hand? How would we be able to take care of Meghan? What disabilities would we face in the future and how extensive? When would we return home? When could I go back to work? Every waking moment these questions swirled in our minds, yet we did our best to ignore the uncertainties and focus on what we had to do to recover and see each other again.

Our search for a rehab hospital finally led us to Treasure Coast Rehabilitation Hospital in Vero Beach, Florida—just forty-five minutes north of Tracey's parents in Port St. Lucie. This hospital had extensive experience with orthopedic injuries, an impressive staff, and state-of-the-art facilities. I was also relieved to learn that their staff plastic surgeon was the former head of the Yale-New Haven Hospital Burn Unit and now headed Treasure Coast's newly developed Burn Patient Rehab Program. In fact, I would be their first patient.

The one factor that provided me with the most hope of complete recovery lay not within the confines of the hospital, but in a small strip mall less than a mile from Treasure Coast. The mall housed the clinic of a talented occupational therapist, Evelyn Rose, a leading authority in the world of occupational therapy and hand surgery rehabilitation. I was thrilled to learn that Evelyn would accept me as a patient and hoped she would be able to restore at least some function to my right hand.

Tracey's discharge from Martin Memorial to Treasure Coast was set for October 28—seven weeks after the crash. I would follow her one week later.

Because my femurs were rodded and had healed so well, I started physical therapy after the sixth week of my recovery. This was a gradual process that began with a unique torture—the dreaded tilt table. A tilt table is exactly what it sounds like. Because one can't just hop out of bed after lying in it for six weeks and begin walking, a more gradual adaptation is needed to gain strength. I would have to walk before I could run, stand before I could walk, and rise before I could stand. Because of muscle atrophy and general weakness, if I just stood up and tried to walk, blood would pool in my legs and I would faint. My muscles needed time and stress (exercise) to accommodate these changes and regain their function before I could even think about walking. So onto the tilt table I went.

Wheeled into a room that smelled like a locker room and looked like a cross between a clinic and a grade-school gym, I was led to a table that reminded me of Frankenstein's gurney. It was a cracked brown vinyl table with a footboard on one end and many straps dangling from the side. I lay on the table, and the therapist pulled the straps tightly across my head, chest, and arms, and a few more across my legs.

The table began its slow, creaking ascent to a shallow angle of less than 30 degrees. I quickly learned why the straps were necessary—my head was spinning, I broke out in a cold sweat, and my body felt like jelly. As blood pooled in my legs and surged into my healing donor sites and grafts, I experienced such intense itching that I had to stop the procedure. It was a sensation nearly as intense as any pain I had experienced throughout my hospital stay—as if my legs were covered with poison ivy and then set upon by thousands of mosquitoes. It was truly unbearable.

My recovery soon progressed from the tilt table to finally standing on my own—with a therapist carefully holding the belt strapped around my waist. Although the itching subsided somewhat after the first several days, it was still bothersome, but now I could at least switch my weight back and forth between my legs and alleviate it somewhat. After a couple of days of standing sessions, I took my first steps with the aid of a therapist—and was surprised and thrilled at how well my legs worked. I could walk! Though my first steps were hesitant and halting, I soon progressed to thirty or forty steps at a time.

Tracey's own adventures on the tilt table would wait until her admission to Treasure Coast Rehab Hospital. And that would only happen after surgery to remove her traction pins and weights—a procedure she looked forward to with both anticipation and dread.

Tracey had the surgery on October 24. It was a relief for her to finally lie free in her bed—the confining grasp of the traction's cables, pulleys, pins, and weights blissfully loosed. Yet she was not entirely free—when she awoke, she found her legs shackled in heavy braces from her hips to her feet. Finally able to move her own legs, she found that movement only came with the greatest effort as she had to fight against the weight of the braces, her own weakness, and searing pain as her muscles struggled to come to life. She had not moved her legs since the night of the crash, and she would now have to fight through storms of pain if she had any hope at all of regaining control over her legs.

The reality of what lay ahead hit her—her legs were nearly useless, misshapen from the many fractures, scarred from surgeries, and nearly as painful as the night they were broken. The long and difficult road before her was quite evident—she knew she would need extraordinary determination, extensive therapy, and God's help to recover.

Tracey endured a difficult transition from Martin Memorial to Treasure Coast Rehab. Still on edge and very self-protective, she tensed with every shake and shimmy of the transfer from her bed to her gurney, throughout the ambulance ride and eventual transfer to her bed in TCRH. It was not a smooth transition and the entire process frustrated her. The most daunting aspect of the transfer between hospitals, indeed the entirety of her hospitalization, was the complete lack of control over her entire situation. Not only could she not control her body, she felt as if she were at the mercy of everyone around her. And the ultimate freedom and independence—walking on her own—was still beyond her immediate grasp and might never become a reality.

I had one more hurdle to overcome before I left Tampa and could see Tracey; I had to see myself. I hadn't looked in a mirror since the crash and knew at some point I would have to confront my new reality. My mom and dad were in my room when I asked for a mirror. Mom hesitated and said, "You have to understand how far you've come since the crash, and if you've healed this well in two months, you'll get even better." Then she added, "Are you sure you want to do this?"

Her hesitation confirmed that the image I would now see would obviously not be the same one I saw before Tracey and I left for our fourth anniversary dinner just weeks before. When I answered "yes," they brought the mirror to my bedside table. I cannot begin to imagine their thoughts when I raised the mirror to look at the injuries that would mark the rest of my days.

I took a deep breath and slowly focused on the marred face staring back at me. My overwhelming emotion was not one of shock or anger, but sadness. If Mom and Dad thought I had healed remarkably in the last seven weeks, I must have endured hideous injuries, because the visage in front of me was certainly not a pleasant sight.

The entire right side of my head, face, and neck was scarred, scabbed, and cherry red—bandages covered my right temple, from the top of my head to my ear and eye. My ear was scabbed and bent, my nose scarred and reddened with a nasogastric tube threaded through it. I had lost most of my right brow, and my burned hair was chopped almost to my scalp. Metal bars on my teeth held my jaws shut, and several lacerations had been stitched from my chin through my lips and up to my nose.

I stared quietly for some time and firmed my resolve to recover. On November 4, I left Tampa General Hospital for Treasure Coast Rehab Hospital. The medical team secured an air ambulance for the trip from Tampa to Vero Beach, and I set off for the next stage of my recovery. Not only was my discharge from Tampa General a milestone in itself, I was going to see my bride. I could hardly bear the wait to be with her.

9

Touched by Angels

Poignant. That is the only word that can singularly describe our reunion that day in November.

In almost every respect, the flight to Vero Beach's Treasure Coast Rehabilitation Hospital was the opposite of my flight to Tampa. I said my good-byes to the staff at Tampa General, thanked Carol for her special care, and prepared to leave with my mom and dad. Where there had once been silent fear as I left Stuart, there was now hope—hope at seeing Tracey once again, reuniting with Meghan and being a family again, and hope that although we were rolling in on gurneys we would walk out on our own. Another big difference—the crowd this time was waiting in anticipation of my arrival, not with dread at my departure.

And what a welcome it would be. By the time of my arrival, Tracey had had a week with the staff, and true to her social nature and evangelical flair, I later learned that virtually the entire hospital staff and the other patients now knew our story and were looking forward to my arrival. In that setting—a rehab hospital, where patients and their families have suffered their own tragedies and heartaches—anything that resembles good news holds great promise to lift their collective spirits and is cause for celebration.

As we landed at the airport, the humid Atlantic air seemed to hold my hopes, dreams, and longing for Tracey aloft as the paramedics transferred me from the plane to a waiting ambulance.

The ten-minute ride to TCRH seemed like an eternity. I simply did not know what to expect. *When will I see Tracey? Will I get checked in first, examined, and then see her? What if she's in therapy and I can't see her immediately? How will she react to my appearance?* I was wracked with more uncertainty, doubt, and anxious questions than the night in La Crosse when I walked with Tracey before our first kiss.

When I arrived at the rehab hospital, I know I looked really awful; nothing had changed since my first glance in that mirror at Tampa General. Additionally, my burned arm glistened unnaturally where it had been grafted, and the fingers and the thumb of my right hand were wrapped in tight bandages, which seemed to highlight my partial amputations. I was sweating and felt like a general mess—not the way I wanted to present myself to my wife.

I looked out the window of my ambulance and didn't see her. I thought that perhaps she was waiting in her room or in therapy. What I did see were scores of faces, like oddly framed portraits in a gallery, peering through every available window and door that faced the driveway.

Emotions swirled inside me as the paramedics took me from the ambulance on my gurney and Mom and Dad wheeled me toward the entrance. Then as we came around a large column I saw her—*Tracey*! We were side by side, facing each other, and could not speak. My mind just fixated on her. Tears clouded our eyes and joy filled our hearts, scarcely believing we were together again. She was so waiflike and looked so wounded, but I was beyond happy. We were together again—that was all that mattered.

The most loving act that has ever been visited upon me came next from Tracey. Still worried and a bit embarrassed by how I looked, she looked at me—and I hope that if I have but one memory left when I die it is this: She looked me in the eyes, reached out her hand, and with a gentle touch, swept her hand tenderly across my scarred face. Then she reached down and grabbed my right hand—the one with all the burns, grafts, and bandages—and kissed the back of it. It was her way of telling me that she loved who I was within and my appearance did not matter. I burst into tears at her tender and loving acceptance.

I will never forget what Tracey did for me that day—it was perfect and beautiful and transcended all the ugliness we had suffered. And best of all, it was completely genuine, heartfelt, and innocent. It was Tracey, my own angel.

We were truly a remarkable sight. Tracey lay in the wheelchair at an almost 45-degree angle to minimize the stress on her pelvis. My mom didn't recognize her at first. When we rolled up to TCRH, Mom remembers thinking, *Look at that poor girl in the wheelchair—so small and all broken up with those big braces on her legs.* She thought she was looking at a girl of about fourteen.

Tracey weighed no more than ninety pounds at that point, and her body was overshadowed by her braces and the large wheelchair. Her hair was cut short, and her lower jaw and face hung at an odd angle. It was only after Mom saw Tom and Mary behind her that she realized it was Tracey.

When I flew from Martin Memorial almost eight weeks before, the tears on the faces of those who saw me off appeared to be washing away our dying dreams. Now they had transformed into tears of joy that seemed to baptize us with renewed hope. From the shared experience of our fiery crash, through the agony and struggle of our recovery, to the quiet beauty of our reunion, Tracey's gentle touch forged in our souls an unbreakable bond.

Our quiet celebration was marked by collective sighs of relief and renewed hope, as if we had each climbed a mountain from opposite sides in a brutal race, with death itself dogging our every step, almost too battered to go on, too hurt to move forward, too exhausted to make it another inch. Yet here we were, finally at the summit, together again—collapsing in each other's arms, entirely satisfied and completely joyful.

It truly was a renewal of our wedding vows to each other. For better or for worse, we would fight this battle together. What our life would become was not yet determined, but it didn't matter as long as we had each other. We would rehab our bodies, our souls, our minds, our marriage, and our lives one step, one day, at a time.

Indeed, this day surpassed our wedding day. That ceremony merely made us husband and wife. Living through this nightmare forged a stronger, unbreakable bond between us, and Tracey's tender touch that day was the gentle seal on our hearts. I love her with my entire being—her heart beats deep within my soul, and I would do anything for her. We are one.

Later that day, as I rested alone in my bed, I heard some quiet voices in the hallway, spilling softly into my darkened room. As the door swung open, I looked up to see Meghan, backlit by the bright hallway lights streaming through the doorway. Gently held high by Leslie-Ann, Meghan was babbling away as they glided to the side of my bed. Tracey's sister placed Meghan next to me.

Somewhere deep inside, the fear that my little girl wouldn't recognize me—or not remember me at all—crept into my thoughts. I was hopeful but wary. *Please, God,* I begged. *Let her be mine again.* The room slowly swelled with more people as Tracey, her parents, and then my parents silently tiptoed in. Meghan's eyes darted around, perhaps feeling the sudden weight of our expectations. She was studying everyone and everything in the room, and as she turned toward me, she hushed her happy babbling.

With a huge lump forming in my throat, I reached out to her. I was so desperate to connect with her again, and my heart ached with fatherly devotion. As I spoke to her through my clenched jaw, the sound of my voice seemed to echo somewhere deep inside. I could almost see her thinking, *Wait—whose voice is that? I think I recognize that voice; could it be . . . ?* As I slowly extended my hand to her, Meghan seemed suddenly buoyed by my touch, as if she were nearing a monumental discovery that she was only now beginning to understand. She became very still and looked closely at me with her big blue eyes—as if mining the depths of my soul. She fixed her gaze upon my every feature. The familiarity of her sweet scent infused my entire being with an intense, tender longing. Raising her left hand to meet mine in a gentle touch, still staring into my eyes, she uttered one simple but incredibly meaningful syllable: "Da!"

My little angel.

My heart melted and giant tears streamed down my face.

I hugged Meghan as desperately and as tightly as I dared. And with that recognition, came a torrent of babbling words and gestures that I could only imagine was her way of trying to tell me all that had happened in my absence. As if she was trying to both comprehend and explain our separation.

Being with Tracey and Meghan again gave me an appreciation and comfort that soothed the tattered edges of my soul. With Tracey next to me and Meghan in my arms once more, the pain and anxiety of our long separation began to melt away. Though not the idyllic dream of almost unlimited possibilities our lives once were, our hopes now were more basic. This was a place where we could begin anew—a starting point from where we could dare to dream again.

10

Baby Steps

As Tracey and I began our rehabilitation, we set our sights on the simple things that we used to take for granted—the ability to walk, to use our limbs, health and wholeness, independence, to work and be rewarded, to be a family—anything that could be considered "normal." The first two months spent in the hospitals had been merely a prelude to gain the strength to begin this new and much longer journey to wholeness.

My first steps came the next day with two milestones—removing the arch bars and wires that kept my jaws together and taking the feeding tube from my nose that seemed, when they pulled it out, as if it extended past my stomach and down to my toes. It must have been at least five feet long! These two events gave me a much-needed surge in confidence and energy. I not only looked a bit more human, I could at last eat and taste food again.

Of the two of us, Tracey had to endure the most difficult physical challenges at TCRH. Her body had been brutalized. Her twenty-some fractures, most of them in her legs, with weeks of lying in a bed, had wasted her muscles and robbed her of strength and stamina. Each day was a test of how much flexibility her knees, hips, and ankles would gain—degree by degree, millimeter by millimeter. With braces stabilizing her legs, her therapists would stand her between the parallel bars while they held tightly to the large gait belt strapped around her waist. They would help her take first one, then two or maybe three steps at a time. Tracey would have to use her entire body to hoist each leg forward in an awkward, exhausting shuffle.

I found it almost impossible to watch her struggle to restore the most basic movements to her once athletic and graceful body. As her husband, I felt I was supposed to help and protect her, to make everything better. My heart ached each time I saw her fight to move a muscle, flex a joint, or take a halting step. Her determination and fortitude carried her forward—I could see the pride in her face with each small victory.

Here we were in the same place at the same time for the same reason, yet as I watched Tracey struggle through rehab, I realized that beyond the physical differences of our injuries, our individual realities since the crash were actually very different, explained, at least in part, by our personality differences and outlook on life at the time.

I was used to adversity, and as I mentioned earlier, for whatever reason had always expected some sort of great trial in my life. Tracey lived with the expectation that life would always be relatively trouble-free.

After the accident and the first weeks of hospitalization, I was either unconscious or medicated to a comalike state and my awakening and realization of what had happened became a gradual acceptance. Tracey's experience and her realization of it were more sudden and intense, almost beyond comprehension. In one moment our life was full of peace and promise, in the next it was pure mayhem and misery, and it was Tracey who felt this most acutely. As I watched her fighting against this new reality, all I could do to help was pray and encourage her. My admiration for her grew each day.

I concentrated on regaining the use of my right hand. The surgeries, amputations, and grafting made it look and feel like it had been soaking in a saltwater bath for two weeks, wrapped with shrink-wrap, and heat-shrunk until it tightly bound up every fiber and bone. My hopes to restore my withered hand now lay in the therapeutic art and science of Evelyn Rose at her hand clinic.

To their credit, our medical team focused on much more than our physical ailments. The doctors, nurses, and therapists set their sights on complete rehabilitation—mind, body, and soul.

While we understood it would be an incomplete process, we did not know how far we could go, what physical abilities we would recover, or what our future limitations might be. We didn't dare to look back; I think we both feared that the destruction of our previous lives would overwhelm us and slow our progress.

We had heard the whispered concerns and prognoses almost from day one: Tracey would never walk, infections would eventually kill me, I would lose my arm, we would be in pain all of our lives, we would never have children again, our marriage would never survive, and on and on. But we were determined to defy the odds and not only survive but thrive.

We thrilled with each step Tracey took, celebrated with every millimeter of movement I gained back in my hand and fingers, and tried not to worry about the overall pace of our recovery or ruminate over the possibility of any long-term disabilities or health problems.

Fresh worries did occasionally dampen each triumph. With every step she took, Tracey worried it might be the farthest she would go. As I gained strength to walk without the aid of a walker or cane, I grew more and more exhausted.

The doctors attributed my fatigue to a number of factors— my overall increased activity, hours of daily hand therapy, additional surgery and grafting on my face and head, not sleeping well, and the general stress of our overall recovery. We had routine blood tests every week and waited with mild trepidation for the results. One afternoon while I was in PT, one of my nurses, Linda, walked up to me with some papers in her hand. "Dann," she said, "there's a little problem with your blood work." My stomach jumped as she continued, "Your liver enzymes are elevated. We need to do some more tests."

Given that this was the late '80s, the fact that we had each had dozens of blood transfusions, and that we were in an area of the country with a somewhat questionable blood supply (southern Florida), Tracey and I were in constant fear of AIDS. With each routine blood draw, we held our collective breath until the results were in. With my lab results now showing a problem, it only enhanced our fear. After repeated tests and more doctor visits, my diagnosis indicated I had acquired what was at that time identified as non-A, non-B hepatitis, now recognized as hepatitis C.

In 1989, hepatitis C was poorly understood and generally considered a low-risk cousin to the more threatening A and B forms. There were no tests to screen donated blood for this particular virus, and if infected, there was no treatment other than time. After several weeks, additional tests indicated my liver enzymes were slowly returning to normal, at which time doctors reassured me that I was "cured." The state of knowledge at that time had showed that even though AIDS might not be immediately apparent, it might show up long beyond the actual time of infection—a concern that would remain with us for years.

Before we knew it, Thanksgiving was upon us, and as another small step in our recovery, the medical staff decided we could have our first "day pass." We would go home for the day to Tracey's parents in Port St. Lucie, about forty-five minutes south of Vero Beach, and return to TCRH that night. We were thrilled at this next step toward normalcy and being with Meghan again—as a family.

We arrived at Tom and Mary's in the middle of a cool gray day amid a warm welcome by Tracey's entire family. After two and a half months in hospitals, it seemed almost surreal to be "home" again—with Meghan and other family members in a real home. Until we were home again with family, even for a few hours, we hadn't realized how much we missed the simple, basic pleasures—having a snack, relaxing in a recliner, moving to our own schedule, and personal privacy. It was a wonderful feeling that highlighted how far we had come and how far we had yet to go.

As quickly as Thanksgiving came, Christmas was fast approaching. While at times the days seemed to drag by, time continued to march on. We tried our best to get into the Christmas spirit, but it didn't really feel like Christmas as we struggled through our daily therapies and watched other patients struggle as well.

One particular night, we thought it might be nice to watch something on TV together. We each had a little four-inch TV attached to a pole next to our bed, so if we were going to watch anything together, we would have to be side by side. Since our beds were about ten feet apart, I simply unlocked the wheels and pushed them together to watch a movie neither of us had ever seen: *It's a Wonderful Life.* By the end of the film, we were both in tears—it was easy to empathize with George, who thought he had lost everything only to have a heavenly angel and dozens of earth-angels come to his rescue in his darkest hour. It seemed a fitting metaphor for our life, both then and now.

Before Christmas arrived, we had two more celebrations— Meghan's first birthday on December 13, and three days later, Tracey's birthday. Given how close we were to missing these milestones, they were especially meaningful to us. My mom and dad flew down to celebrate with us and we were able to spend the night at Tom and Mary's, our first night out of a hospital since the crash. Even though it was just one night, we cocooned ourselves with Meghan in the utter relief of "normal" and took yet another step forward.

For Christmas, we would be home for two full days. The only gift I wanted for Tracey was to get her wedding ring fixed. Hers had been badly damaged in the crash. It was twisted almost into a figure-eight and several of the small diamonds were missing. I couldn't imagine how they got it off her finger without cutting it. Even if it meant melting it down and remaking it, I wanted Tracey to wear her original ring. It seemed symbolic to me that if we could restore her wedding ring, we could somehow restore our lives.

On a day trip to a mall, I managed to sneak away from Tracey to see several jewelers. Showing them the ring and explaining our story, only one would take on the challenge of a repair. One week later, the jeweler called and, somewhat cryptically, told me, "I did the best I could. Please come and check it out." Tracey's brother Rob drove me to the mall, and when the jeweler showed me the ring, the wry smile on his face foretold the result—it was beautifully restored, looking more gorgeous than I remembered. I took out my wallet and he refused payment, saying it was a gift and that he hoped that Tracey and I would enjoy many blessings from this point on. His work and generosity overwhelmed me.

A few days later, surrounded by family opening gifts, Tracey opened her gift and burst into tears when she saw the ring. She put it on her finger, and it sparkled with more brilliance than the Christmas tree. The gleam in her eye shone as bright as the lights. It was another step toward wholeness.

Being home with everyone for the long Christmas weekend was a wonderful break from the daily grind of the rehab hospital. And as we prepared for our return trip, I looked at Tracey and said, "I don't want to go back there. I like being home with Meghan—I wish we could just stay." Tracey looked at me with sad eyes. I knew she felt the same way, but always the voice of reason, she responded, "I do too. I really do. But the more time we spend at the hospital the sooner we'll get back home—for good." I knew she was right, but I dreaded going back.

After Christmas, our recovery proceeded at a steady but agonizingly monotonous pace. We were not only fighting physically to heal, we were also fighting mentally. Maintaining a positive attitude was vital to our recovery. So many times throughout our ordeal, attitude drew the fine line between life and death, recovery and stagnation. We built our attitude with faith. We knew there was a reason God spared our lives, and we recognized that He can create blessing from any circumstance. Whatever additional blessings He might have in store for us, we wanted to participate as fully as possible. Now that we had defied the odds and survived, we still needed that attitude to remake ourselves and keep up our daily resolve.

Physically, we measured our progress in terms of degrees of movement, steps taken, weights lifted, and stamina, pain, and exhaustion overcome. Our mental and emotional states were assessed by the medical team as well, but with much less specificity. One of their primary concerns was our long-term mental adjustment to our new reality. No matter how good our care or how much we pushed ourselves, there would come a time when we would have progressed as far as we could and the difference between our past and future physical abilities would show a deficit.

Tracey and I were determined to do our very best and not allow any disability to inhibit us in any way. Wishful thinking, perhaps, but for us it was the only way to move forward.

In addition to the physicians, nurses, and therapists, our medical team also included psychologists and social workers. One of their top concerns was another potential consequence of our injuries—a shattered marriage. They knew that the divorce rate among couples where a spouse has a chronic illness or disability is, by some estimates, as high as 75 percent. Much of our counseling focused on the difficult transition to our new reality and the stress that illness and disability put on a marriage. Facing exhaustion, infirmity, and other debilities would require constant vigilance lest they obliterate the blessings in our life.

We understood their concerns but weren't really worried. We had the best possible support a couple could have—God. And our wedding vows were not just ceremonial dressing to us. We did—and do—take them seriously. Moreover, given the circumstances of how we began our relationship, we always felt that we had an "arranged" marriage, arranged by God. Truly, what God brought together, no one, not a drunk driver, our injuries, or anything else, could tear asunder. Our faith in God and our faith in each other kept us going then, and now.

Soon after Christmas, Tracey was walking, though haltingly, with the aid of canes instead of a walker, and I had left my wheelchair and walker behind for good, only occasionally using a cane. I had regained more movement in my right hand, and it now seemed not a question of *if* I would regain useful function, but rather *how much*. Our daily therapies concentrated on regaining movement and strength. It was now only a matter of time before we would be discharged and receive our therapies on an outpatient basis.

With my rehab progressing well, the medical team estimated my discharge for shortly after New Year's Day, around January 5, 1990. Before her discharge, Tracey still needed additional weeks of therapy.

However, I refused to leave Tracey's side, even for a few weeks. With all we had endured, there was simply no way I was going anywhere without her. After careful consideration, the medical team eventually agreed on a compromise—they would keep me an additional two weeks and release Tracey a week early. Our discharge date was set for January 19, 1990—144 days in the hospital since our crash.

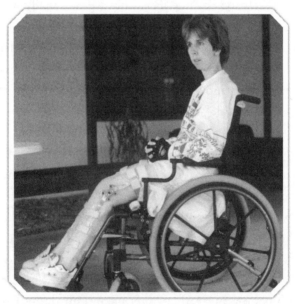

Tracey, while at Treasure Coast Rehabilitation Center, December 1989, three months after the crash

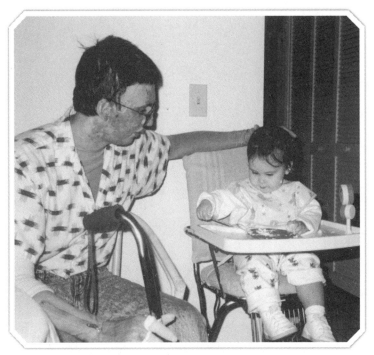

Meghan and me during a home visit,
December 1989

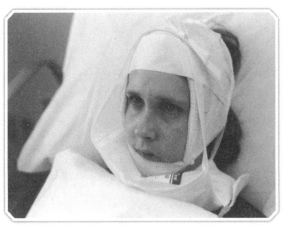

Tracey
after major
reconstructive
jaw and facial
surgery

11

Home Away From Home

Tracey and I entered Treasure Coast Rehab on stretchers. We walked out on our own two feet.

I cannot exaggerate the significance of our accomplishments. Where walking once seemed an almost impossible goal, we were thrilled to reach such a gigantic milestone on our road to normalcy.

Still, formidable challenges and many unanswered questions lay before us. We knew there might be additional surgeries, but we didn't know how many or when. No one knew if Tracey would walk without the aid of a cane, or worse, if pain or other circumstances would make walking again impossible. The chief physician at TCRH wrote in my discharge notes that it was unlikely I would ever regain full-time employment due to the extent of my trauma. Could I work at all? When would that happen? How would we pay our bills? How would we handle the duties of full-time parents? Would we ever be able to live alone without help? How would we react to the world outside our protected confines, and how would the world react to us? How would we interact with each other again after these many changes? Could the psychologists and social workers possibly be correct? That we'd have a difficult time in our marriage after everything we had endured?

The slow-burning fuse ignited on the night of our crash continued to smolder with uncertainty. Answers would have to wait; if we tried to overcome the doubts and uncertainties that flashed through our minds all at once, we would wilt under the sustained heat of adversity. Instead, we faced each challenge on its own, one moment at a time.

Weeks before our discharge from TCRH, we decided, for many reasons, to stay in Port St. Lucie, Florida, with Tom and Mary for the next several months of our outpatient rehab. One large factor was that it was midwinter back home in Wisconsin and the thought of traveling back and forth in the snow and ice was more treachery than we cared to face. We also wanted to stay close to our medical teams to maintain the continuity of our care. Additionally, Tom and Mary had the time to help us with things such as taking care of Meghan, driving us to our many appointments, and assisting with everyday tasks.

Tracey, Meghan, and I were together again at last, and we relished the idea that we were finally becoming whole again, a functioning family—even with our limitations. It was sheer joy to be with Meghan on a daily basis, regain our privacy, and be able to function and breathe with some overall normalcy.

Even with Tom and Mary's help, our new routine was every bit as exhausting, perhaps even more so, as in the rehab hospital. By early February, it was painfully obvious that it would be months before we could truly be on our own again. The reality tempered our optimism, but we took it in stride—knowing that we would take one day at a time, hope for the best, and fight as hard as we could to get our lives back, whatever that might mean.

Another adjustment I had was the long-term treatment of my grafts and burns. It can take months or even years for skin grafts and burned skin to heal and mature. When normal skin is injured, collagen lies down in an orderly fashion, healing the damaged areas. With burns and grafts, the skin loses its natural pressure and the collagen produces a patchwork of jumbled tissue that builds up and causes additional scarring. To aid in my recovery, I had to wear pressure garments that help the skin repair.

I had a full jacket and gloves for my upper body and leggings for my lower body. Due to the heat, I could not wear the head and neck garment—I would sweat right through it and have to remove it almost immediately. Dr. Hart had a solution. Rather than wearing the face mask, he would instead inject steroids in the many scars on my face and neck. Steroids deplete the skin of collagen, blocking the buildup of scar tissue and helping to flatten the scars.

Every other week I would make the trip to his office and receive dozens of small injections in the scars on my face, head, and neck. Even though each injection felt like a bee sting and would leave my face reddened and swollen for a couple of days afterward, they were still preferable to wearing the face mask. And the results were dramatic. After many months the scars had flattened and faded.

While our therapies continued and we made steady progress, Tracey's jaw needed additional attention since those fractures had not healed correctly. Her jaw was misshapen and her bite was misaligned. This would be an extensive surgery. The surgeon would carve her upper jaw to recant the angle at which it met her lower, re-break and reset her lower jaw, and reshape her chin to accommodate the other changes.

In May, we returned to Martin Memorial for the surgery. It lasted well beyond the predicted four hours. I was terribly worried, but soon a nurse came out to tell us that the surgery was finished and Tracey would soon be in her room. We retreated there, and after waiting another couple of hours, we finally heard the chattering of her gurney as the orderlies wheeled her to her room.

I was unprepared for what I saw next. Tracey's entire head was swaddled in ice bags, and what portion of her face I could see was bloody and swollen.

I cringed at seeing her in such obvious distress. Even after all we had been through, neither of us had really witnessed the other's hurt at this level. This was so fresh, the wounds so raw—I could barely stand it. I felt helpless, angry, and sad. I stayed with her through the night, doing my best to comfort her and make sure the nurses did everything possible to help her.

Tracey slowly recovered over the next few weeks, but I could not shake the brutal image of her after the surgery.

We had both done our best to minimize our injuries, but seeing Tracey like that was a wake-up call to the difficulties that might lie ahead. Still, we renewed our resolve and did everything we could to further our recovery.

Even with the setback of her facial surgery, Tracey's overall progress was astounding. With nearly sixteen fractures from her pelvis to her knees, and a left ankle crushed so badly that it was nearly amputated, merely walking again was a miracle. She was walking, but would likely never run. She had a permanent limp that would only marginally improve, and pain would be a daily companion, worsening as she got older. Her future, no matter how well she healed, would eventually be filled with pain and stiffness from the corrosive burn of arthritis.

My progress was more straightforward. My walking had steadily improved since my first steps in Tampa. My burns, scars, grafts, and donor sites all continued to heal nicely, but I would have to continue to wear the pressure garments. My right hand had improved dramatically, and while I would never regain the dexterity I once had, I could do many everyday things I used to take for granted—shaving and brushing my teeth, and gripping tools, a steering wheel, cooking utensils, and the like.

We tried not to worry about the future, and did our best to live as Jesus taught: "Tomorrow will take care of tomorrow." It would be years before we could say, "Okay, we've healed as much as we can; we've gone as far as we can go; now we just maintain what our repaired bodies have become." We did wonder if that moment would ever arrive, but what could we do except continue to fight and never surrender?

Our recovery gradually shifted to maintaining the activities of daily living, gaining strength and stamina, and becoming independent again. We both knew what our next step would be—to go home to Wisconsin. I knew Mary dreaded our leaving. She was extraordinarily family-oriented, sometimes to a fault, and after the accident it seemed she almost could not abide the thought of not being with Tracey, as if Tracey would not get better without her. I understood her feelings and reluctance to let go, but also knew the reality of our situation.

We still had our duplex in Wisconsin. We had renters to attend to, and though we could not live there ourselves again because it was a two-story, we could rent our side out to help pay the mortgage. Additionally, Syntex Labs had magnanimously allowed my position to remain open for as long as it would take for me to heal. Although my TCRH discharge notes contained doubt about my ability to return to work, I knew I would eventually work again.

I also knew Mary understood that at some point we had to return home. What concerned me far more was Tom's reaction to our leaving. He was too diplomatic and understated to raise any objections; I knew he supported us and fully understood why we had to return. However, I never lost sight of the fact that Tracey was his youngest daughter, and that alone would make our parting very difficult for him.

But what caused me to toss and turn in the weeks before we left was Tom's relationship with Meghan. Since the night of our crash, Tom had been the cocoon that had kept Meghan safely ensconced within. Their bond had grown so tight that I feared their separation would be emotionally devastating for Tom.

The crash had already burned through the carefully woven tapestry that once blanketed our families—masking our collective insecurities and vulnerabilities, and that fuse continued to smolder. The sunny illusions of a life without tragedies or hardship had vanished in the acrid smoke of our wreck. Our parents had done so much for us; they'd sacrificed, they'd worried, they'd agonized, and I recoiled at the thought of causing any one of them further pain; I knew our separation would be difficult no matter when it happened.

As Tom and I talked one night in early June, I eventually broached the subject. "Tom, you know we've come to a point where we have to consider going back home."

"I know," he replied softly.

"You know that I can never repay you for everything you've done for Meghan and for Tracey and me—you've been a real blessing," I said. Then I added, "I would love it if we could all live close to each other, but we have a life to get back to in Wisconsin. We have our house, and I still have a job waiting for me."

He hesitated briefly, just long enough to take a deep draw on his cigar—his thoughts seeming to hang in the air with the smoke. "Well, I can't say that I won't miss you guys. Meghan has just been a doll, a real doll, but we'll only be a flight away. I understand that you have to go back. You need to go home and get your lives back." Then he added, "Look, if you don't go back home, you'll always feel like you just kind of fell off the face of the earth."

He was right, and until he phrased it that way, I hadn't realized that was exactly how I felt. The previous September, we had left Wisconsin for our vacation in Florida, and we never returned home. As far as our life back home was concerned, it was as if we had just disappeared. I was greatly relieved by his gesture. It was classic Tom—realistic, honorable, and giving.

12

Echoes

We eventually chose June 28, 1990, as the date we would return home. With our two-story house unsuitable for us, more surgeries ahead, and still needing help with Meghan, the obvious solution was to live with my parents in their ranch home, just a few miles from our duplex in Jackson.

We left Florida on a bright, sunny Thursday afternoon amid tears and well-wishes from Tom, Mary, and Tracey's entire family. Our parting was indeed sweet sorrow. And we arrived at the Milwaukee airport to tears and cheers of family and friends there, led by my mom and dad. The crowd was so large and boisterous that the other travelers must have thought we were some kind of celebrities. For all those who gathered to welcome us back home, I guess we were.

The trip from the airport to my parents' home in Jackson was almost dreamlike—everything we passed had the bright aura of newness, but still seemed washed with the dull sameness of familiarity. We were living through our own state of déjà vu, but it was very real—and equally surreal.

During those first few days, the euphoria we felt as we stepped off the plane continued as we reacquainted ourselves with our hometown and visited with friends and family. It lasted until we gathered the courage to go back to our own home. Walking into our house again was like stepping through a time warp. We had only been gone ten months, but when we left, Meghan was a babbling baby. Now she was a talking toddler. Where our path in life was once clear and direct, our path now was muddled and uncertain. When we locked the door behind us as we left for Florida, we were healthy and vibrant. Now as we unlocked the door upon our return, we were injured and weak.

As we stepped over the threshold, a sudden, overwhelming sense of loss sucked our breath away and settled heavily on our hearts. As the songs and dreams of our previous life echoed around us, shadows of our once idyllic existence danced around every corner, and the memories clung to us like spider webs as we turned through each doorway. The home that once burned bright with desire now haunted us with dreams unfulfilled.

Even recognizing what we had lost, we also understood how much we had gained in the last ten months. Our recovery was far better than anyone could have expected, and we would just keep pushing forward for as long as we were able. But before we could live on our own, we had to overcome a few more obstacles. Meghan was nearing two years of age and, like most toddlers, required constant attention. We had more surgeries that hindered our efforts to keep up with her, and while Tracey and I stayed busy with our therapies, my mom and dad were needed to watch Meghan.

We were both on crutches at various times throughout the next several months; Tracey needed additional surgery on her ankle and foot and I had the rods removed from each of my femurs in separate surgeries. By spring of 1991, though, it was clear that we were ready—finally—to be on our own again.

As much as we looked forward to our independence, we knew we were going to miss the help that our parents had provided throughout the past years. It was more than just picking up the slack when Tracey and I were too disabled or too tired to take care of Meghan—it was their unflagging belief in each of us that helped inspire us on those occasions when our world looked dark and uncertain, when our hope waned and despair clouded our judgment.

So on March 1, 1991, we moved into our own apartment, ready to take our final step to full independence. We were just a few miles away from our duplex in a new apartment complex in Jackson—mere minutes from my parents' house. It seemed almost like a halfway house—we were on our own but help was nearby if we needed it.

It was exciting. We were ready to blaze a new trail, discard the damage wrought in our lives, and begin anew.

13

A New Life

It had been a year and a half since the crash. In the last three years, Tracey's family had moved to Florida, we had bought a house, had a baby, been gravely injured in a car crash, survived dozens of surgeries, spent four and a half months in hospitals, lived with Tracey's parents in Florida, and then my parents in Wisconsin, and were now on our own in an apartment. The winds of change that twisted like a tornado through our lives fanned the flames of a firestorm that threatened to immolate all that we knew and held dear. Our ability to adapt, persevere, and overcome was constantly tested.

Finally independent, our future seemed brighter with each passing day, but the one question that still loomed largest in our minds was when, or if, we could add to our family. The doctors in Florida warned Tracey against getting pregnant again, fearing it might be too much for her body to handle. From the stress on her fracture sites and joints, to problems with blood clots, to concerns (however remote) about a dormant AIDS virus arising from the blood transfusions, there were just too many unknowns. While their concerns about a future pregnancy seemed entirely reasonable in the months after the crash, her doctors seemed almost deliberately vague about long-term concerns.

Although we were not anxious to conceive anytime soon, we did not have definitive answers regarding pregnancy and were eager to make a determination one way or another. Tracey and I visited her obstetrician, and after discussing her history since the crash and reviewing the medical records from Florida, he sat us down in his office and began to discuss his prognosis. His look of concern foretold what he would say.

"I'm not all that worried about your fractures. They've healed nicely and a C-section would take care of those concerns, if that were a problem. What does concern me are the blood clots you had when you were in traction. Everywhere you had a clot, your body made scar tissue at those sites. Pregnancy raises the risk of blood clots, and they could be life-threatening."

Tracey's eyes welled up as he continued.

"What I'm saying is that if you did get pregnant, I would consider it a high-risk pregnancy, very high risk, and I would recommend against it."

I interjected, "If this were your wife, what would you tell her?"

"Exactly what I'm telling you; I wouldn't let her do it."

We were both crestfallen. The smoldering fuse of destruction and doubt threatened to burn us yet again. We walked in silence as we left the office. Tracey broke down when we reached the car. "The accident took so much from us. We lost all that time while Meghan was a baby, we lost our health, we lost our house, and I lost my job. All I wanted was to have more kids—I just want to be a mom."

She was right, and there wasn't much I could say to comfort her. This was one of the few times since our ordeal that we acknowledged what we had lost. However, we both realized that focusing on our problems rather than our blessings was a sure ticket to bitterness and anger. We did not want a life of regret and disappointment. That would be no way to live, and we could not ignore the blessing we already had in Meghan. We owed her a life lived to the fullest. If God wanted us to be a family of three, we might not understand it, but we would accept it. Whatever direction our life took from that point forward, we would trust God to guide us.

Just a few months after we moved into our apartment, I finally felt ready to return to work. I was biking, lifting weights, and jogging—albeit slowly and painfully—and I finally felt strong enough for the demands of daily work.

Returning to work was a huge step. Sales is a highly visible profession; I would be interacting with dozens of people every day, and I was still sensitive to the looks and stares my scars and grafts sometimes brought. My right hand is gnarled and disfigured, and the right side of my face is grafted and scarred. As I have aged, the scars have matured and are not as noticeable. But back then it was a constant worry for me. I sometimes felt utterly naked in public.

My first day back, May 1, 1991, began with a sales meeting. Tracey drove with me that morning and walked me into the meeting room. Most of my co-workers were also my very good friends, so coming back was more than just another day at the office—it was also a celebration.

After a twenty-month absence, we felt like we had finally climbed back on top of the mountain, having conquered many of the challenges forced upon us. As the team welcomed me (us) back, I saw reflected in their faces and smiles the many blessings God had bestowed upon us since our ordeal. It was not only that we knew angels had been there to help us and heal us that night, but that out of our tragedy God had blessed us in so many other ways. What else could we ask for?

The life we had embarked on years earlier was slowly returning to us, perhaps not in every detail and not without some concessions, but our life was reaching a sense of normalcy again. After all the trials and struggles we had endured, anything close to normal was a victory.

As much as we reveled in vanquishing all the obstacles that were once in our way, we could not ignore reality. Tracey's injuries prevented her from returning to work, and she could not run after Meghan, which was especially terrifying, considering a two-year-old's propensity for running off. Our battle with chronic pain continued as well. I struggled with bouts of fatigue that would drag me down for hours, even days at a time. Fatigue is still a cross I bear.

Our lives seemed to be in a constant state of change, but each change signified a distinct improvement. After several months in our new apartment, we thought about where we might build a house we could call home again. We bought a lot in the nearby town of Colgate, and soon settled on our ideal house plan, chose a builder, and broke ground in November 1991.

Our new house would be a sprawling ranch home with everything on one floor. We wanted every room and necessity within easy reach, with wide halls and doorways. As we watched our home rise from the ground and eagerly anticipated moving in the summer of 1992, the thought that the three of us would be alone in a home at least three times the size of our apartment was almost incomprehensible. Since Meghan was born, we had either lived in the small confines of our duplex and apartments or crowded in with our parents in their homes. Having all the extra space of a new home seemed almost foreign to us.

And the extra space filled us with thoughts of a brother or sister for Meghan. Of course it also brought the nagging concern of Tracey's obstetrician's advice against another pregnancy. I had trouble understanding why her history would be associated with such great risk.

We sought the advice of a local specialist in high-risk pregnancies, Dr. Anderson. We brought in Tracey's mountain of medical records and her own obstetrician's notes. After a thorough review, he began to explain how dangerous pulmonary embolisms could be, mentioning many of the same risks that Tracey's obstetrician had almost a year earlier.

"Wait a minute," I interjected. "I understand how deadly a pulmonary embolism can be, but Tracey has never had a PE."

Dr. Anderson looked puzzled. A serious-looking but affable man with a hint of gray at his temples, he frowned and said,

"Your obstetrician has in his notes that you had a pulmonary embolism after your accident."

Tracey shook her head, "No, I had fatty emboli from my fractures and I also had some blood clots in my left leg, but I never had any clots in my lungs—at least none that I'm aware of."

"Hmm," Dr. Anderson mumbled as he began thumbing through Tracey's records from Martin Memorial. After several minutes his demeanor changed a bit and a warm smile spread across his face. "I think I see the problem. As far as I can tell, when you had your fatty emboli, some notes in your chart referred to them as *pulmonary*, but now I see that they later corrected that." He went on, "If this is correct, and what you're saying holds up, I see absolutely no problem with a pregnancy. I would still recommend daily heparin to keep your blood thin because of the deep vein thrombosis (DVT)." Then he added with a bright grin, "But if you want another baby, I think you would be fine!"

Now we both had tears in our eyes. One of our greatest misgivings had suddenly evaporated. Maybe we could have a larger family after all. We knew God's timing is always better than our own, and perhaps we would indeed be blessed with another child when the time was right. The thought of moving into a new home *and* having another baby left us almost breathless. Our future suddenly seemed to burn with promises as bright as ever.

14

A Rock, a Reprieve, and a Rebekah

We moved into our new home in June 1992. We were thrilled. I felt like our house was a rock upon which we would be building the rest of our lives—raising our children, taking care of each other, and growing old together. It provided a wonderful sense of permanence and belonging.

We had been hoping Tracey would be pregnant by the time we moved in, but apparently the time was not right. Meghan was conceived just weeks after we decided to try, so going nearly a year without any results was particularly frustrating, especially for Tracey. After several months of consultations and fertility tests with various doctors, we almost gave up hope. We were already sick of doctors, clinics, and all things medical after our lengthy recovery, and the fertility treatments and testing began to feel like more drudgery.

Rather than asking for God's blessing and waiting in humble patience for His answer, it seemed like we were begging God to give us another child. However, like Jesus' story about the persistent widow in Luke 18, we did our best to remain faithful and patient, in the hope that God would eventually answer.

By late fall, we turned our attention to the upcoming holiday season and all but resigned ourselves to our family consisting of just the three of us. Tracey found herself deep in prayer one day and a flash of insight came to her like a bolt of lightning. Feeling like God was speaking to her, she felt an unexpected warm rush throughout her body that came with this thought: *Tracey, it is not your timing, but mine.*

I still recall the excitement in her voice as she recounted her experience. She was convinced we would conceive, if not soon, then at a time God would deem best for us. Completely at peace after this experience, Tracey's anxious worry about another pregnancy vanished and she continued to prepare for our first Thanksgiving and Christmas in our new home.

By Christmas we got the greatest present possible—we were pregnant. Tracey's due date was in August. Our life was all smiles as we felt the richness of God's blessing.

Yet for all the joy of Christmas 1992, we would soon discover 1993 to be yet another tumultuous year—one that would leave us smiling, crying, sighing with relief, and dazzled by God's blessings again and again.

We had hoped Tracey's pregnancy would be smooth and uneventful, but it was not to be. I had to give Tracey daily shots of heparin to prevent blood clots—she feared needles but braved the injections as the price to pay to keep well during her pregnancy. Thankfully, she never developed blood clots, but her health wasn't perfect, either. Early in her pregnancy, Tracey became ill with a severe gastrointestinal illness that required several trips to the hospital. We soon discovered why she had become so sick. Nearly half the population in the Milwaukee area suffered from the most massive outbreak of waterborne illness in U.S. history—cryptosporidium. We had been in Milwaukee the day before she got sick. A sip of water from a water fountain was all it took.

By June 1993, Tracey, Meghan, and I were traveling to Nebraska for her cousin Michelle's wedding. Michelle had asked Meghan to be a flower girl and of course both Tracey and Meghan were thrilled. Growing up, Tracey had spent many Christmases, Easters, and summer vacations with Michelle and her younger siblings, Erich and Beth. We would be joining Tracey's parents in Nebraska and looked forward to the wedding and reunion.

We met Tom and Mary at the airport in Lincoln, rented a car together, and headed to Fremont for the weekend's festivities. Though we had a great weekend, I was worried when I noticed that Mary was extraordinarily pale and appeared tired, taking frequent naps and resting more than usual. By the time the wedding and other gatherings had ended, Mary reassured us that she was feeling fine and was merely battling an extended bout of bronchitis and a cold. Like many smokers, Mary appeared to have a weakened immune system that made her especially vulnerable to such maladies.

After the weekend, we didn't give Mary's health another thought. We were busy preparing for our baby Rebekah's arrival and ensuring that Tracey remained healthy. Just a few weeks later, I got a phone call late one night from Mary.

"Dann," she began. "I would've called Tracey first, but with her being pregnant, I would like you to tell her something for me." She hesitated and then said, "I have some bad news to tell you—I have lung cancer."

"I'm so sorry you have to go through this," I answered. "You know I love you and Tom—what can I do to help?"

"Well, just break it to Tracey as gently as possible. Don't worry about me—just take care of Tracey and the baby."

Mary's appearance in Nebraska now made sense. The cancer had likely been smoldering for months, a slow burn that was robbing her of oxygen, stealing away her energy and vitality. Her pale appearance was due to internal bleeding from a very large tumor.

Because of Mary's familiarity and trust in Community Memorial Hospital in nearby Menomonee Falls, where she had worked for nearly thirty years, she said she would be "coming home" for her surgery and treatment. She asked if it would be okay if she and Tom stayed with us for the duration of her treatment. I had already assumed they would.

Tracey had been out for the night, and I agonized over telling her the news. It had only been four years since our accident, and in many ways we had not yet fully recovered—some wounds still felt fresh.

When Tracey got home, I waited for her to sit down, but my demeanor alerted her that something wasn't right. "Something's up—what's wrong?" I told her that her mom and dad would be coming for a visit and then why: "Tracey, your mom has lung cancer." I winced, waiting for the torrent of tears and grief that I knew would follow. Instead, Tracey just closed her eyes for a few moments and then resolutely said, "Well, whatever happens, we'll just deal with it." She called her mom, shared some tears and a quick prayer together, and then made some initial plans for their arrival in the next few days. After she hung up the phone, Tracey looked at me and said, "I don't know why I'm saying this, but I just feel like everything is going to be okay."

She was obviously in denial—Mary had been a heavy smoker for almost forty-five years; she had been coughing up a lot of blood, and her doctors in Florida told her that the tumor appeared to be quite large. The survival rate for lung cancer was only about 10 percent and she was already symptomatic, a dismal sign. I was glad that Tracey was so optimistic; at seven months pregnant, she certainly did not need this additional stress, and anything she could do to reduce her anxiety over her mom's condition was fine with me. As much as I hated the thought, I fully expected that Mary would be gone within the year, if not sooner.

Tom and Mary arrived just a few days later. We put them up in our spare room, and suddenly our house became the center of the universe for the entire family and their close friends. Our home was part crisis-management center, part restaurant, and part hotel.

Mary's surgery was set for July 1, 1993. As family and friends waited out the days before her surgery, the unspoken fear that hung over all our conversations was that Mary's eventual death was a foregone conclusion. The only mystery left was waiting for the surgeon and oncologist to tell us how long she had. Still, everyone did their best to maintain their optimism and petitioned the Lord for His intervention and healing.

On the day of surgery, we waited anxiously as the doctors began their arduous task. As the hours dragged on, nearly two dozen family members and friends were sprawled throughout the waiting area. Some watched TV, others read, and still others of us nodded off as we waited for news of Mary's progress.

Dr. Jenks, her primary surgeon, suddenly appeared in the lobby. Momentarily stunned by the throng that seemed to engulf him, he took a step back and then recovered. Looking for Tom, he found his worried face and spoke directly to him. "Mary's doing pretty well. We removed two-thirds of her right lung, and along with it, a grapefruit-sized tumor and several lymph nodes."

Collectively, our hearts sank. This was an ominous sign. He went on, "She's lucky, though. Her tumor was encapsulated. But—" he raised his hand as if to emphasize—"the initial pathology report shows that it was small-cell lung cancer. This kind of cancer is very aggressive; in most cases, we don't even operate on these tumors because they grow and spread so quickly. But because this was so large and she was bleeding, we really had no choice. The fact that it was encapsulated gives us some hope. We'll know more after the nodes have been biopsied and we get the rest of the pathology report." He ended with a sigh, anticipating the rush of questions that peppered him.

The surgeon seemed to simultaneously ignore and yet answer all of the questions, not replying to anyone specifically. "She's in recovery—a nurse will let you know when she gets to her room. We really won't have an accurate prognosis until we get the full report, and we won't get that for a couple of days." We thanked him, and as he walked away, he added, "She's very fortunate."

A cautious wave of relief washed over us. For now, the news filled us with hope. Small-cell lung cancer was the worst cancer she could have—the five-year survival rate was less than 1 percent. Yet the fact that it was encapsulated was promising. Still, the tumor was large and that seemed to worry Dr. Jenks.

Over the next several days, Mary gradually regained her strength. The pathology report confirmed everything Dr. Jenks had told us; it was indeed small-cell lung cancer, the tumor was encapsulated, and her lymph nodes, almost beyond belief, were free from any signs of cancer. After spending several days in the hospital, Mary came home to rest, recuperate, and gain strength as she prepared for the radiation treatments her oncologist prescribed.

One week after Mary left the hospital, a follow-up CT scan of her internal organs shocked our collective mood with a dreadful result—Mary's right kidney held a tumor about the size of a golf ball. Mary's oncologist and surgeons immediately scheduled surgery to remove her kidney. The hope that had buoyed our spirits after Mary's lung surgery seemed suddenly to evaporate—lung cancer frequently metastasizes to the kidneys.

The news devastated all of us. If the cancer had indeed spread, Mary's prognosis was grim—maybe less than a few months to live.

Mary's surgery to remove her right kidney took place on July 28. In a scene that largely repeated itself from her lung surgery four weeks prior, the entire family again waited anxiously. Tracey was now almost full-term, and I worried constantly how this stress was affecting her, but she waited with a calm reserve, again deciding that the best course was to take one step at a time, neither worrying too much about what seemed like the inevitable nor hoping too much for a miracle that would again spare Mary's life.

A nurse came to us in the waiting room and asked us to come in to a nearby family counseling room. Since it was so small, only the surgeon and Tom were inside the room, with the rest of the family spilling out into the hallway and crowded around the door.

The surgeon waited for everyone to assemble and become quiet. "The surgery went just as we planned—we removed her right kidney without any problems and it did have a large mass almost in the very center." He continued, "Now, we won't be sure until the final biopsy is complete, but—it really is quite remarkable." He paused and seemed to stumble on his next words. "The tumor *appears* to be benign. She's doing well, she really dodged the bullet."

Amazing. Simply amazing.

It had seemed all but certain that this cancer would hold Mary in its unrelenting grasp until it took her last breath. She should not have lived even six months beyond her first surgery, and yet she not only defeated her cancer, she lived far beyond what her prognosis should have been.

This was yet another lesson for Tracey and me to rely on God's grace to hold us up and keep us strong through life's firestorms. It also reaffirmed our belief in the power of prayer—Mary's history, symptoms, and type of cancer virtually guaranteed she would die from it. We prayed and God granted our request; it is as simple as that.

Any question that God had a hand in Mary's victory over cancer was answered some months later when she told us about an experience she had in church.

Before her surgery, one of Tom and Mary's first stops after settling in to our home was to visit their family church where they had been members for more than thirty years—St. Francis Episcopal Church. Coincidentally (or not), St. Francis was holding a Healing Service and Holy Eucharist on the Wednesday night after their arrival. As Tom and Mary sat quietly in the church, she said a sudden peaceful calm seized her and seemed to bathe her entire being.

A bit later, parishioners lined up for a special healing blessing by Father Peter. When Mary reached the altar, the priest recited the blessing as he anointed her head with oil. He and the deacons next to him then placed their hands on Mary's shoulders, and as he concluded with "in the name of the Father, Son, and Holy Spirit," Mary said a sudden feeling of warmth surged through the right side of her body "like a fire" and lingered for several moments. The sensation caught Mary by surprise; she'd neither expected nor immediately understood the warm sensation.

Mary was always a bit of a conundrum—an intensely private person who was nevertheless honest and forthright in her opinions. She held on to this particular event with the small hope that perhaps, just perhaps, she had just received a powerful answer to everyone's prayers. Yet she would not share this event with any of us, lest false hope lead to unrealistic expectations. As she said, "Maybe I just imagined everything—maybe I was just hot because I was so anxious." Still, it did give her hope, and it allowed her to relax before each of her surgeries. Mary waited until her treatments were finished before she finally opened up and told us about her healing in church on that summer night in June.

I do not question it at all. While I am certain that many explanations could be proffered, taking into account the entirety of Mary's situation, it seems all but certain that the only way she could have survived her cancer was by divine healing.

Mary was still recovering from her surgeries when Tracey went into labor on her August 19 due date. Our life had been such a whirlwind, and here we were again—at least this event was one of celebration and awe.

Meghan's delivery and birth had been long and difficult; this one was quick and relatively easy. Just a few hours after Tracey was admitted, she gave birth to another healthy baby girl—Rebekah! We were overjoyed; we now had a happy, healthy family of four, and Meghan was thrilled to have a sister. Again, God had prevailed in our lives; He led us through some dark days of uncertainty and doubt to the promise of His forbearance and light.

We would need His steadfast love one more time just a few weeks later. Rebekah was five weeks old and thriving. Tom had become her chief caretaker, as he let Tracey and Mary recover and gain strength over the weeks following Rebekah's birth, while I worked. One evening after I had just returned home, Tom picked up Rebekah from her cradle, looked at Tracey, and said, "Tracey, she's burning up!" Tracey hurried over and picked up Rebekah to feel the fever burning throughout her tiny body.

I grabbed a thermometer. A quick read showed Rebekah's temperature to be 105 degrees. We rushed her to the hospital and could only watch as Rebekah cried in agony as vials of blood were drawn from her tiny veins, and worst of all, as a yellowish fluid dripped from a large needle inserted through her spine—the much feared spinal tap. There are many sights a parent never envisions for their child. A spinal tap is definitely on that list.

Rebekah's pediatrician, with whom we were casually acquainted, walked into the room and recognized us immediately. His reaction describes how far and wide our reputation for misfortune had spread. Turning to the nurse who had walked in with him, he said, "Oh my—it's the Stadlers. These poor people have been through hell."

As much as we appreciated his empathy, we were anxious to hear Rebekah's diagnosis.

"Rebekah has viral meningitis," the doctor announced. "I know that sounds frightening, but even though we cannot treat viral meningitis, it is far preferable to bacterial meningitis." He went on to say, "While bacterial meningitis can cause brain damage or death, viral meningitis is rarely associated with any long-term problems. We'll keep Rebekah for a few days, treat her with antibiotics just to be safe, and make sure she recovers without any problems."

We were, of course, greatly relieved. We had endured yet another crisis and received another answer to our prayers. We had long ago learned to trust the Lord in all aspects of our life—no matter how great or small—and we would not be disappointed. We really had no choice other than to live by faith. Try as we might, we had very little control over our lives.

Over the next three years, Rebekah grew into a happy, healthy toddler, Meghan's grade school years were off to a promising start, and Mary had completely recovered from her cancer. Though our life had seemed to stabilize, some nagging problems continued to whisper hints of struggles ahead. Fatigue continued to dog my every step, and my facial injuries led to problems with my sinuses that required several additional surgeries.

Nevertheless, a pattern had emerged in our lives. Though we consistently found ourselves enduring one hardship or calamity after another, the numbers of which appear beyond statistical probability, we would turn again and again to the Lord. When we were at the end of our endurance, patience, and faith—if not our sanity—we placed our hope and trust in the Lord, and He consistently delivered us from our most feared consequences. Angels and miracles cooled the slow burn of the fuse that wound its way through our lives, extinguishing the small fires that seemed to erupt and clearing the smoke that clouded our future.

15

Agony and Angels in Nebraska

What Might Have Been

Late on Friday night after Thanksgiving 1996, our phone rang. On the other end I heard Mary's distressed voice. "Dann, I have something terrible to tell you. My niece, Bill's daughter, Beth, and her husband, Chris, were in a terrible car accident in Nebraska—they were both killed. Their daughter, Emily, was in the car also. She has a fractured skull, but it looks like she'll be okay." In circumstances disturbingly similar to our own, Tracey's cousin Beth and her husband, Chris, a young couple with a young daughter, were traveling unfamiliar roads while on vacation.

It was crushing news. Their car had slipped on an icy road on their way to Chris's parents in Ewing, Nebraska. They slid directly into the path of a pickup truck. Their small car stood no chance. The only survivable space was the small area in the back seat where Emily had been securely strapped in her car seat.

Tracey was devastated. Growing up she had spent many vacations with Beth and her other Nebraska cousins, including Michelle, whose wedding we attended three years earlier.

Beth and her husband first met not long after she graduated from high school. Their attraction overpowered them both. Beth was the young, pretty girl with a playful spark in her eye, and Chris, four years older, was the handsome and irrepressible "college man" with a dynamic, charismatic personality. They soon became inseparable and also something else—expectant parents.

At only eighteen, Beth was pregnant. Chris—the only son of Dennis and Cathy, cattle ranchers who are two of the most commonsense and decent people you could ever hope to meet—was initially terrified at having to face their parents. Nevertheless, after the shock of their announcement wore off, Chris soon found them supportive of their plans to finish their education and get married. Beth and Chris dearly wanted to be responsible parents that would provide a loving and stable home for their daughter.

Chris completed college and wanted to become a teacher, and Beth went to school to become a dental hygienist. Two years after they had Emily, Chris and Beth walked down the aisle of St. Patrick's Church in Beth's hometown of Fremont, Nebraska. After having started their relationship under difficult circumstances, their future was as bright as it could be.

A mere five months later, Tom, Mary, Tracey, and I were in Fremont in the midst of a dark and gray winter's night that seemed to choke us with the grief that hung heavily in the air. We had arrived on Sunday night at the funeral home just as they were finalizing preparations with the families for the funeral the following Tuesday.

We could only watch as Beth's parents, Bill and Pat, and Dennis and Cathy grieved for their lost children—their pain too raw to soothe, their heartache too deep to heal.

Sharing the anguish suffered by everyone in that small room, Tracey and I were overcome with the realization that we were witnessing what could have been our own deaths seven years earlier. The parallels were too strong to ignore—a young couple just starting out, a young daughter, and a terrible crash. But while Tracey and I lived through our injuries, Chris and Beth succumbed to theirs. It was almost more than we could bear; we were not only grief-stricken at the loss of Chris and Beth, but the surreal feeling that we were participating in what could have been our own funerals swept over us.

Another strong feeling accompanied our grief—a feeling we'd never anticipated and had never before experienced— survivor's guilt. We felt like we were on display, where everyone was looking at us, trying to understand why we'd survived such an awful crash, while Chris and Beth did not. We wished we had an explanation, but of course we did not—and that made us feel even more uncomfortable.

We knew this almost unbearable tragedy was not about us, and we didn't want it to be. While we were careful not to interject ourselves in any way beyond that as grieving family members offering support, our own accident came up repeatedly in conversation and we were frequently introduced as "the couple that was in that bad car crash in Florida several years ago." Or friends, relatives, and acquaintances would ask us about the accident and how we were doing. It got to the point that Tracey and I often retreated to our hotel room.

Despite our attempts to remain as silent witnesses to the grief surrounding this tragedy, it gradually dawned on us that perhaps we could impart a small measure of comfort in the midst of the pain. On the night of their accident, I wrote a poem about Emily that I later gave to Pat and Bill. Apparently moved by my words, they asked me to read it at the funeral.

I was touched by their request, but certainly did not want to read my poem without Dennis and Cathy's approval, and in the course of our discussion, I briefly told them of Tracey's near-death experience. Though I knew nothing but time and God's mercy could ultimately help heal their hearts, I felt incredibly drawn to them and hoped that Tracey's story could somehow assuage a small part of their grief—and perhaps would one day bring them a measure of comfort.

Even as we found ourselves in the midst of this nearly unbearable tragedy where they had lost their only child and daughter-in-law, there was an incredible peace, love, and warmth that seemed to radiate from both Dennis and Cathy. They welcomed us into their lives at that moment, and it was completely genuine. They are such an understated, yet dynamic presence that we consider ourselves fortunate to call them friends after all these years. When I read the Beatitudes, I think of Dennis and Cathy.

They listened intently to Tracey's story and seemed to embrace the meaning of it, with Tracey explaining again that she could not possibly know what they were enduring and that we did not want to intrude in any way on what was a very private time of mourning. Doing her best to describe the Lord's peace, love, and beauty she felt during her brief glimpse of heaven, Tracey emphasized that this was just the beginning of what Beth and Chris must also have experienced, and so much more awaited—and would for all eternity. She explained that though she did not understand why Chris and Beth were taken, she knew they were both in heaven and would somehow be watching over Emily. They seemed grateful for Tracey's insight and her words of reassurance that Chris and Beth were in the presence of the Lord.

Though time had seemed to stop, suddenly it was Tuesday, and we found ourselves at St. Patrick's Church for the funeral. St. Patrick's was a beautiful old redbrick church that seemed to rise out of the earth itself, as solid as the bedrock of its own citizenry. As we entered through the huge wooden doors, our eyes fixed upon the expansive interior of the church; the rectangular nave was divided by a lengthy aisle that stretched to meet the magnificent altar. On either side of the aisle stood majestic columns that reached up to a grand, soaring ceiling, with each column seeming to reach for heaven itself.

The beauty and majesty of this setting that just a few months before had borne witness to the celebration of Chris and Beth's wedding now appeared at odds with the presence of grief. Still the grace and solemnity of the church were appropriate, as they seemed to mollify the heavy hearts of all who filled the pews. It seemed as though the entire town of Fremont, if not all of eastern Nebraska, had filled the church.

The proceedings began, and the two caskets were somberly carried side by side to the front of the church, the hushed murmurs of the grieving blending with the deep tenor of the tolling bell. As Father Mike began the service, I admired his composure. Having counseled Beth and Chris before their wedding and performed the ceremony, he was clearly shaken by their deaths, but he was a rock of faith and a true leader to this flock.

Just before the Gospel reading, I read my poem. Though I wrote it in the first person singular, I wrote from the viewpoint of Beth and Chris's parents.

Emily's Gift

I saw you last night
In a million stars and dreams
You were deep in my heart, yet . . .
I could not hold you
I could not touch you
I cried for me
I cried for the whole world
You are everywhere I am
Yet you are still not here . . .

I am with her now
Your little angel that God blessed us with
And I feel you through her
Your smile
Your laugh
The sparkle in your eyes

And I feel your touch
Your love . . .

And though my love lies bleeding
Like rose petals upon the new snow
She shows me
That through the windows to her soul
Are glimpses of yours and . . .
For the briefest of moments
Our souls have touched and then . . .
I know, I feel it burn in my heart and soul
You are not gone
You are just away, just away
And I will be with you again
For I love you always
I love you forever

As I returned to my seat, I looked at Tracey and marveled at the look of peace on her face. Though one of the most emotional people I have ever known, in the midst of this tragedy she was completely calm. On the other hand, I am not usually one so emotional and yet I felt within me a rising tide of sadness that I could barely contain.

Tracey and I joined the gathering at Beth and Chris's grave site, and the crowd's muffled cries and hushed sighs hung heavily in the frigid air. I could barely keep myself composed. Though already lost to eternity, I could not bear the thought that once their crypts were sealed, they would be lost to their daughter, Emily, for all time as well. In retrospect, I think part of me was crying for how close Tracey and I were to the same fate; part of me was crying for the pain both Chris and Beth must have felt leaving Emily behind, and part of me was crying for Emily.

The stark reality that Emily would now grow up without her mom and dad was beyond my ability to comprehend. In a switch from our usual roles, Tracey did her best to comfort me—and I again marveled at the obvious strength of her faith. She was peaceful, calm, and strong.

After the last grains of earth fell softly upon their graves, we left the cemetery and retreated to the sanctuary of our hotel room where we could rest until we went to the post-burial wake. I dropped Tracey off at the hotel entrance and parked the car. Still heavy in my own despairing thoughts, I walked up to our room and opened the door.

When I saw Tracey, an incredible sight slammed into my soul. Her face was alive. There was a luminous glow like an alabaster radiance that defies earthly explanation.

In shock, I stood just inside the threshold as the door softly swung shut behind me. "Tracey, what happened? Your face is glowing." I continued to stare at the light beaming from her face. It conveyed such a deep sense of peace that it overwhelmed me. She just looked at me with a smile of utter contentment.

"Please don't tell anyone this," she replied. "I don't want to make this day about anyone other than Beth and Chris." I agreed, and waited for her explanation. "When we were in the church, as I was listening to the priest and looking at their caskets at the front of the church, I was thinking about how empty their bodies were. While we were all so sad, they were not there—I knew they were exactly where they should be, with God.

"When I turned to tell you that, I glimpsed something out of the corner of my eye. Toward the ceiling I saw an angel.

He didn't look like my angel, the one I saw after our crash. This angel was enormous and he filled the entire upper part of the church with his wings spread out above everyone—like he was gathering and holding the entire congregation in his wings, comforting them. He was beautiful. Then he turned his head toward me and our eyes met; his eyes sparkled—almost as if he was winking. It seemed like he was acknowledging me. He smiled at me and I knew that everything was going to be okay—that Chris and Beth were exactly where they're supposed to be."

I listened intently, and from the conviction of her words to the glow on her face, I knew that every word she spoke was the absolute truth. The heaviness that I had felt in my heart just moments earlier vanished as it met the sincerity and peace that seemed to come from the very depths of her soul. I was awestruck and wanted to shout her experience to the world.

"You have to tell everyone about this," I told her.

But Tracey repeated her earlier admonition. "Please don't tell anyone, at least not now. I really don't want to make this about me—it's about Beth and Chris and their families."

Just at that moment, Mary walked into our room. Never one to tread lightly, she almost slammed the door open and slightly startled us as she now filled up the doorway. Stopping suddenly and looking directly at Tracey, in her gruff voice she simply said, "You're glowing! What happened?"

Closing the door, we sat Mary down, and looking at Tracey, I said, "I'm telling her!" Tracey just rolled her eyes, resigning herself to the fact that her secret would now be impossible to keep under wraps.

After sharing with her mom exactly what Tracey had told me, Mary just nodded her head in agreement and said, "Well, I came up here to tell you something." A few minutes before, as she and Uncle Bill were talking in the lobby of the hotel, he told her that one of his friends rushed up to him as the burial service was concluding. She turned him around, pointed toward Tracey, and asked him, "Bill, who's that woman over there, standing next to the man with the dark hair?"

Tracey and I were standing in the middle of the crowd, so she could not have known what our relationship was to Bill or anyone else. Bill, of course, immediately recognized Tracey and told his friend, "That's my niece Tracey, with her husband, Dann. Why?"

She explained, "I first noticed her in church, and I've been watching her." Shaking her head, she added, "I'm not sure what it is, but there's just something very special about her." She was not alone in noticing Tracey; she was but one of many that asked Bill about Tracey that day.

Postscript: After a recent conversation with Chris's mom, Cathy Vandersnick, she informed me of an unexpected letter she received in 2000 from a paramedic who assisted at the scene of Beth and Chris's crash in 1996. It is reprinted here—

Dear Cathy and Denny,

Thanks again for your excellent Christmas card. It is always nice to hear from those of you who we've been able to assist at our ambulance scenes. We were so sorry for the deaths of Emily's parents, and we have to deal with that from time to time.

It's nice to know you appreciate the efforts of our ambulance crew and fire dept. [and what they] have done, and we're grateful for it. I also feel Emily is greatly blessed to have you for her care.

One thing I always wanted to tell you, was that the night we went to the accident scene, someone was there already holding Emily. She was a younger lady with dark hair and glasses. I thanked her for helping, and she stayed there until Emily was taken care of. I believe in angels and I know she was [the one] there that night. No one was able to get her name or address. The Good Lord always comes through.

Merry Christmas,
Kevin

16

A Fire Within

Of the many small, smoldering fires that have affected me since the night of our crash, perhaps the most challenging has been fatigue. At times it is so debilitating it almost hurts. I remember one particular week in Michigan where, as part of my job's continuing education requirements, I was part of a group that followed a surgical team. My exhaustion was such that I not only thought I might pass out, I actually hoped I would. It would at least get me some rest in one of the hospital's beds.

One factor cited by doctors for my fatigue is that I have suffered chronic sinus infections almost continuously due to the many fractures in my sinuses and face, having had four additional surgeries since the crash to repair various anomalies and clear my sinuses for improved drainage and breathing. While the surgeries have helped, I still have the chronic sinusitis and it leads to frequent headaches, infections, and fatigue.

I also have post-traumatic fibromyalgia, another frequent source of fatigue. Finally, chronic pain is exhausting as well—the mental and physical toll that pain exacts from both Tracey and me is difficult to quantify because we have lived with it for so long. We really do not know what it is like not to have pain. It's a daily battle.

As these trials continued in the years after our accident, I also paid special attention to the possibility that my previous case of hepatitis C might come back to haunt me. Hepatitis C's long-term ramifications are better understood now than they were in 1989. This includes the possibility that it can lie dormant for years and suddenly return, becoming a chronic infection that can lead to cancer or eventual liver failure and death.

Though the crash had occurred nearly a decade ago, the indiscriminate fuse of peril continued to slowly burn, and that fuse was now poised to find a cache of powder hidden deep within my body, threatening an explosion that could shatter our lives.

About once a year, I had specific lab tests to assess my liver enzymes, watching for a meteoric rise in my lab work, which would indicate the virus was no longer dormant. By 1997 a definitive test for the hepatitis C virus finally became widely available, a ribonucleic acid (RNA) test that looked specifically for the virus's genetic material in a patient's blood. I had the test as soon as it became available. It came back positive—I now had a confirmed case of chronic hepatitis C. One of its hallmarks is fatigue. With chronic sinus infections, fibromyalgia, and now hepatitis C, it was no longer a question of why I was fatigued; I felt it was more a question of how I ever managed to stay awake.

Over the next several months, I had two liver biopsies, other additional tests, and a great deal of worry that I may have transmitted the virus to Tracey or the girls. Additional testing finally determined that they were free of the virus, but I remained vigilant. We dearly wanted other children, and although I had not passed the virus, it was not a risk we could continue to take. It was a difficult and sad reality that our chances of having other children were essentially over.

After consulting a hematologist at the Medical College of Wisconsin, we learned that chronic hepatitis C is an insidious disease; it leads to more cirrhosis than alcoholism, causes liver cancer, is a major cause of disability, and is the number one reason for liver transplants. If not treated successfully, it can eventually lead to death. We decided that my best chance for long-term health and survival—pegged at just 50 percent—would be a yearlong course of antiviral therapy. Like similar chemo-type treatments, the list of side effects included nausea, hair loss, anemia, psychiatric effects, itching, fatigue, fever, and chills, to name a few.

In April 1999, I began my therapy—and vomited three hours later. Over the course of the following year, I injected myself with interferon three times a week and took ribavirin capsules twice each day. It was just the beginning of an arduous battle that would see me plummet to depths I had never before experienced.

Although my therapy began somewhat ominously—getting sick within just hours of my first dose—I did not notice any other extreme effects in the ensuing days and weeks, with relatively infrequent instances of vomiting. Instead, each injection seemed to produce a sort of mini-flu the following day—a general run-down feeling, achy, with a low-grade fever, but never quite bad enough to be completely incapacitated. I felt like that much of the time anyway, so in the beginning it was difficult to distinguish between the therapy's side effects and my having another off day due to my other problems.

The ribavirin's effects were more subtle, likely contributing to the interferon's fatiguing side effects and further suppressing my appetite. I found that if I spaced the interferon on Monday, Wednesday, and Saturday nights, I could enjoy my Fridays and Saturdays without as many problems, since my side effects seemed worse the day after each shot.

By summer, my appetite regressed to the point where I was rarely hungry anymore, and I only ate because it was time to eat. When I did eat, my portions were smaller and I felt unusually full.

As weather allowed more time outdoors, I noticed that my stamina had deteriorated quite significantly. Where I once could battle through any fatigue and power through a Saturday afternoon of mowing the lawn, other landscaping chores, and general household repairs, I no longer had any stamina or reserves left to fight through my exhaustion. I also began to sleep later and later in the mornings; previously I would wake up early and go for a bike ride or enjoy a cup of coffee before Tracey and the girls woke up. Now I would sleep past 8 a.m. and shun coffee, as it seemed to upset my stomach—and I love coffee.

Every day felt like I was hiking over a mountain. However, regular checkups showed that I was responding to the therapy, which was enough to keep me going. By late summer, the therapy began to exact more of a toll. Although I continued to work, there were days when I was so spent and exhausted it took almost herculean efforts to leave the house.

By February, I had almost no energy reserves left—everything I did took an incredible effort. Just waking up and getting ready for the day was a major endeavor. On some of the days following my interferon injections, I would sleep solidly until 3 p.m., too exhausted to get out of bed.

It was also about this time that the psychological effects of my therapy became more problematic. The therapy was such a slow, grinding process that these effects were imperceptible at first, building slowly over time and then becoming more troubling. I had almost no ability to concentrate, was mildly confused at times, and bounced between extremes of depression and anxiety that left me riding an emotional roller coaster.

Although in retrospect it is easy to see how much I had declined, when I was in the middle of the physical and emotional exhaustion it seemed difficult to identify any single issue that was more problematic than the others—physically or mentally. I couldn't tell the difference between exhaustion and depression. I vividly recall having bouts of extreme panic for no apparent reason and I would retreat to my bedroom or office and fervently pray for relief.

Although the psychological and mental effects of the therapy are now quite well known, in 1999 these effects were just beginning to be understood. There is a phenomenon known as "riba-rage" that refers to the depression, irritability, and anxiety that comes from the combination therapy of riba-virin and interferon. There were times I felt like I had lost my grasp on reality and it was all I could do to remain as calm and deliberate as possible as I attempted to go about my daily activities.

Finally, Tracey had become concerned enough that she demanded a follow-up visit with my doctor. They decided I had endured enough. I had come within just a few weeks of completing the entire forty-eight weeks of therapy, my response seemed complete, and further therapy would almost qualify as torture—I just could not take it anymore. I was finally done!

Gradually, my appetite, energy, and stamina began to improve and the fog mostly lifted from my brain. Even so, I still feel I have never quite recovered my mental acuity after that year of treatment for hepatitis C. I've had problems with concentration and attention deficit disorder (ADD) all of my life, but they were always mild annoyances that I easily dismissed. Since that year of therapy, however, these problems have continued to vex me. They aren't disabling, but there are times when I feel as if my mind is occupied with some kind of mental thunderstorm—with thoughts flashing in and out of my brain—derailing me for hours on end.

In the end, though, my therapy did result in a complete cure. I no longer have hepatitis C, and it is a huge relief to know that I am no longer living with the time bomb of eventual liver failure or cancer. That slow burn has been extinguished, and I remain thankful.

17

God's Special Delivery

One of the most disheartening aspects of my hepatitis treatment was that it likely spelled the end of any further attempts for Tracey and me to have more children. The side effects of the medications were far too risky. Further, Tracey and I were thirty-seven, Meghan was eleven, and Rebekah six. By the time I finished treatment and cleared the effects from my body, it would be at least another two years before we could possibly expect to have another baby.

We had been bitterly disappointed with two miscarriages after Rebekah, and had been through all the fertility work-ups and treatments we could stand—it just was not happening for us. We were overjoyed with the two daughters we had, but as time went on, I found myself more and more perplexed as to why God would not grant our fervent requests for another baby. My relationship with the Lord was such that I felt He had blessed me with nearly every faithful request I had ever asked of Him. I had been almost begging God for a third child—that Tracey would conceive "just one more time." He seemed to be ignoring me, or so I thought, and we had resigned ourselves to our family of four.

Although Tracey had previously urged me to consider adoption, the process seemed so lengthy, expensive, and full of unknowns that even after praying about it, I couldn't imagine adoption to be the path for us.

The very week that my therapy ended in mid-March, I was lying on the couch one evening when the phone rang. Tracey answered. It was her sister, who was working then as a nurse at the local hospital.

"I work with a woman here whose teenage sister-in-law is pregnant and due in July," Leslie-Ann said. "She wants her baby adopted by a Christian couple." Aware of Tracey's interest in adoption, Leslie-Ann then got to the purpose of her call. "I thought about you right away. Are you interested?"

Tracey's heart skipped a beat, but trying to temper her excitement, she said, "I'm not sure, let me talk with Dann."

After she hung up the phone, Tracey explained the reason for Leslie-Ann's phone call. After discussing this for the next few minutes, a sudden silence came upon us and it was as if a veil lifted from our eyes, mine in particular. We slowly looked at each other, and I think that was when God touched our hearts.

"Dann, what if this is what God wants for us?" Tracey asked. "Isn't this another one of those coincidences that is just *too* coincidental? We've been praying about this, your therapy just ended, and now we get this call out of the blue." She added, "I really think this is meant for us; I think this is God's plan." Already I could feel the previous walls I had built up against adoption begin to crumble.

Tracey hurriedly called Leslie-Ann for more details. Her friend's sister-in-law had specific requirements of the prospective couple for their baby: They must be Christians—she must meet and approve of them beforehand—they must have other children so her baby would have a brother or sister, and they must be financially stable. This "coincidence" was indeed far too meaningful to ignore. As we discussed this opportunity, our excitement grew. It was at that moment that I believe Tracey and I considered ourselves as expectant parents for the final time.

The next few weeks were a whirlwind. We first spoke with Anna on the phone, each answering the other's questions, trying to get to know one another—probing gently for any hint of doubt or insincerity. Then we met Anna and the birth father in person. For our part, we had to determine if Anna would see this very difficult and emotional process to the end; was she emotionally stable and mature enough to handle this? We did not want to pour our hope and love into an empty promise, and we did not want to raise hope and excitement in Meghan and Rebekah only to have them crushed.

Our conversations with Anna went far better than we could possibly have hoped. We not only felt completely at ease with one another, but we found great admiration and likability. Far from being a detached act of giving her baby away, Anna showed this was an act of pure love. Recognizing that she was too young to provide the best possible future for her baby, she instead sought a happy, loving, and complete family.

It was clear that this adoption was going to proceed, and with the child's birth just four months away, time was spinning rapidly. We had to hire an attorney and engage the services of an adoption organization to oversee the entire process. There were interviews, assessments, medical insurance, and other arrangements and preparations to complete.

Although there are no requirements for a couple to conceive and become parents, adoption is a rigorous process whereby complete strangers and "the system" ultimately decide your "suitability" to be a parent. There are hundreds of laws and regulations one must heed to complete the process. It is a humbling experience to have every aspect of your life under a microscope.

Every interaction we had with Anna was so positive that we came to regard her with a fondness and tenderness that made her seem almost like a daughter to us. Her maturity and sensibility were remarkable. Though she knew the adoption process, birth, and ultimately surrendering her rights would be tremendously difficult, she was determined to give her unborn child the best future she could possibly provide. This completely selfless act of love—for her unborn child and for us—would be a tremendous gift, and we remain forever indebted to Anna and eternally grateful.

It is amazing how God works and equally amazing how blind we can be to His plans. This blessing showed us that the years we spent regretting what we perceived as God's indifference were a waste. In fact, His plan was far beyond our capacity to imagine, and it was perfect. My hepatitis C was cured, I had finished a difficult year of therapy, He knew that ultimately Anna needed a stable Christian family for her baby, and He knew that this baby was the perfect addition to our family. Moreover, adoptions can take years to arrange—ours happened within weeks. This baby's deliverance to us would be every bit as miraculous as Meghan's and Rebekah's births and as profound a blessing as the other miracles God had worked in our lives. What a glorious example of the manner in which God can turn incredible difficulty, disappointment, and even catastrophe into blessing and joy.

Soon enough, all of the preparations were completed and we found ourselves sweating out the hot summer while waiting for the newest addition to our family. We could barely contain our growing excitement. Meghan and Rebekah were giddy as they helped Tracey prepare the new nursery—fully decorated and stocked with diapers, bottles, tiny baby clothing, baby blankets, and all of the other newborn necessities.

Anna's due date came and went, and our excitement seemed almost as unbearable as that summer's heat. Finally, a full two weeks after her due date, the doctor decided Anna was to be induced on July 23. Tracey and I met Anna at the hospital early that morning and eagerly awaited any news of the pending delivery. Days before, Anna had one more gift for us that we can never repay—she asked us to be present in the delivery room as she gave birth to our child. This humble act was more than we could have possibly asked—allowing us the joy of having our child delivered right to our waiting arms. To be there as our baby drew its first breath was an incredible privilege.

We began the day full of hope and joy. Not knowing the baby's sex only added to our excitement. As the morning dragged into the afternoon, our anticipation was nearly intolerable.

As the evening approached, our excitement grew to concern about the toll the day was taking on Anna and the baby. Our anxiety was increased by the fact that Anna's pregnancy was considered high-risk because she was a carrier of group-B strep, a frequent cause of blood infections, meningitis, and pneumonia in newborns and a significant cause of infant mortality. Nevertheless, we were reassured they were in good hands by Anna's pretreatment with antibiotics, monitors constantly checking both hers and the baby's status, and the fact that St. Mary's had an accredited neonatal unit with an outstanding reputation.

Fully dilated, Anna finally reached hard labor about 6 p.m. This was such a different experience. With our first two children, I watched and waited as Tracey lay in bed, doing my best to comfort and support her. Although Anna had her best friend in the delivery room to do that job, I still felt an almost fatherly devotion to her and wanted to take a more active role, but the best I could do was just hope and pray that all would be well.

I was also mindful of Tracey's reaction—her previous deliveries being as the patient. Now she understood the helplessness that fathers feel as they see their wives struggle through a long and painful delivery. I kept a careful eye on Anna, Tracey, and the medical staff that suddenly seemed to be everywhere.

As Anna grew more exhausted from the constant contractions and pushing, the doctor and nurses became increasingly tense. I also noticed the fetal heart monitor indicated the baby's heart rate was plummeting lower and lower with each contraction. Finally the head appeared—but the monitors buzzed, indicating the infant's distress. The umbilical cord was wrapped several times around the baby's neck, and she became lodged in the birth canal. With alarms piercing through a long and otherwise desperate silence, time froze before the doctor was able to free the cord. Finally, our daughter was delivered—Emma!

I shouted and jumped for joy, but as I came back down, my heart sank with me to the floor. Emma was completely flaccid, blanched white and not crying; there was nothing—no movement at all. She appeared to be stillborn.

Tracey and I were in utter shock and disbelief. The nurses immediately whisked Emma to a corner of the room. They cleared her airways and began working frantically. They inserted long tubes down her throat, calling her name, and then hooked up a respiration bag. Still not breathing, a nurse picked Emma up and raced her down the hallway, disappearing behind the doors to the neonatal intensive care unit (NICU).

Tracey and I followed the nurses and looked through the glass doors. With three nurses and another doctor now working on Emma, the sudden realization that we might lose her before we ever had a chance to hold her seized our hearts and sucked the air from our lungs. We had already given so much love to her—the thought that we were witnessing her death was more than we could bear.

Tracey and I stared at each other in stunned disbelief, tears spilling from our eyes. Our legs gave way and we collapsed against a wall in the hallway. Holding on to one another for support, we sank to the floor.

Suddenly, I recalled a verse from an old hymn I had encountered years earlier in Norman Vincent Peale's book, and a paraphrased version echoed in my head: *"So long hast thy power kept me, surely it will lead me on."*

I looked deeply into Tracey's wet eyes and said, "Tracey, God would not have brought us this far to abandon us now—everything is going to be all right." I just knew He would not have ignited this fire in our hearts only to see it extinguished now; it was the moment of faith we both needed to reset our resolve and reaffirm our trust in God. He would deliver Emma from death's grip straight into our arms, and in an echo from Tracey's angel years previously, everything would indeed be "all right." We held firmly to one another and prayed as desperately as we had ever prayed for anything in our lives.

We stood and turned our attention back to the frenetic activity in the NICU. Emma was a maze of tubes and IVs as the doctor and nurses continued their frantic but purposeful efforts huddled over her tiny body. It seemed like an eternity since she had been born, but only about seven or eight minutes had passed. Then we witnessed an amazing and miraculous sight—Emma moved her arm! And then her legs were wiggling. Next we heard her muffled cry—and we cried with her.

After several more minutes, a nurse came out to advise us on all that was happening. They could not explain why Emma had such difficulty, but after they got an IV in and administered medication and fluids, she finally took her first breath. For now, a respirator would continue to assist her breathing until she became strong enough to breathe reliably on her own. They initially feared her problems were caused by a group-B strep infection. Whatever the reason, the fact that she was now very much alive was all that mattered to us. We put our hope and trust in God. He was in control, and we felt an overwhelming peace and comfort that Emma would be fine.

Emma's Apgar scores were 0 and 1 at one and five minutes. This means Emma was born with no detectable pulse, no breathing, poor color, no muscle tone, and no reflex or response to stimulation—essentially lifeless. That she would survive was a testament to the work of the doctors, nurses, technology—and most certainly to God in answer to our prayers.

Finally we were allowed in the NICU to touch and hold Emma. To finally see her up close and look into her eyes, see her breathing, even if assisted with a respirator, and touch and talk to her was reassuring. We prayed over her, and one of the nurse practitioners who had helped revive Emma walked over to us, asking if we were Christians.

Acknowledging that we indeed were, she informed us that she was a deacon in her church and asked to pray with us. This incredibly meaningful act further enhanced our sense of peace that everything would be all right.

Unfortunately, not all of the medical professionals shared our optimism. One of the first things the doctor told us after he had finished stabilizing Emma was that because they could not be certain how long Emma had been starved of oxygen he was unsure how much damage had been done. He said it would be days, weeks—even months or years—before the nature and extent of damages might be known.

The adoption process is fraught with legalities, and it was clear that the medical team and hospital staff were at a bit of a loss as to how they should proceed. Incredibly, we had social workers and other hospital personnel telling us we didn't have to follow through with the adoption, since the strong likelihood of brain damage or other problems could well put Emma in the special-needs category.

It made no difference to us. The thought of not taking Emma home was unfathomable. She was our daughter, and we would love her and accept her no matter what her condition was or would be. Had Meghan or Rebekah been born with special needs, we would never have abandoned them at the hospital, so in our minds there was no question as to how we would proceed. We loved all three daughters long before they were born and welcomed each into our world with the same tenderness, devotion, and sense of awe. Emma was accepted and loved by us from the moment our phone rang in March, and walking away from her now was a repugnant thought. God had delivered her to us, and we accepted this amazing gift of life that would expand our family.

Tracey and I spent the next ten days at the hospital with Emma, staying night and day with her. Our hearts ached as she had to endure test after test as the team did their best to assess her every bodily function.

As the days dragged on, Emma passed every crucial test and milestone. Soon enough, her sisters and grandparents were able to see her, and then other family and friends came in to welcome Emma to our family and the world. We were especially honored with some special out-of-town visitors, Dennis and Cathy Vandersnick. Their comfort and support in this trying time seemed somehow to close a long circle that began so many years before in those dark days in Nebraska when we first met them after they lost Chris and Beth. When they visited Emma in the NICU, we introduced them to the nursing staff as Emma's grandparents—an honorary title—and we were thrilled to have them with us.

Emma's steady improvement led to her discharge after ten days. She would need an apnea monitor for the next thirty days and neurological testing for the next five years. Though we readily agreed to those requirements, neither of us expected that Emma would have any permanent problems from her difficult birth. God had first performed a miracle in bringing Emma to us, and another in saving her after a nearly tragic delivery. God does not "undo" miracles.

Welcoming Emma home was an incredible celebration of love and acceptance. Our family of four had grown to five and we felt utterly content and satisfied, as if the missing piece we had been seeking for so long had finally fallen into place, completing our family. We quickly settled into the routines of feedings, diaper changes, naps, and attending to all the other needs of a newborn. Meghan and Rebekah were tremendously helpful and excited by their roles as big sisters, and we soon found that a family of five is, roughly, about five times busier than a family of four!

As Emma grew and surpassed every milestone, we almost never worried about her development. Our only concern was that her forehead appeared to be growing in a slightly asymmetrical manner. The right side appeared as if she had hit her head quite hard, leaving a lump that would not diminish. We ignored and dismissed it for several months until she was almost a year old.

In June 2001, my mom was baby-sitting while I was at work and Tracey was visiting her sister Susie in Florida. When I returned at the end of the day, Mom sat me down and with a worried look told me, "I don't want to alarm you, but I've noticed a huge change on that bump on Emma's forehead—it's really getting much larger."

I knew we had been dismissive about this problem, almost hoping it would resolve on its own. "You've seen that much change?"

"Absolutely—it's noticeably larger. Have you asked her doctor about this?"

"We pointed it out at her last checkup, about two months ago, but they said she was probably just sleeping on her head wrong and it would even out after a while."

"Well," Mom said, "it's not getting better, it's worse."

I knew my mom was right. Since my parents saw Emma intermittently, it was much easier for them to notice what they saw as an obvious change. The protruding area had never appeared so pronounced. It was now at least half the size of a golf ball, sitting on the right side of her forehead. I immediately called and made an appointment with our family physician for the next afternoon.

I worried myself sick the rest of the night and could not wait to see the doctor. The next day, we walked into the exam room and I explained my concerns and how my mom had noticed a huge change in a short time. He hadn't seen Emma recently, and I could tell he was concerned as well. He took several measurements and concluded that the difference was glaring enough that he suspected she might have craniosynostosis—a condition where the bones in the skull fuse prematurely and can be a sign of underlying developmental problems. He referred us to a pediatric neurosurgeon for a definitive diagnosis.

I was beside myself with worry. With Emma's history, this could signal the possibility that she had indeed experienced some brain damage at birth. In addition to the possibility of a host of serious medical problems, the surgery to correct the skull deformity seemed too horrendous to consider. Essentially, the surgeon would have to carefully remove her skull, carve it up to new proportions, and reassemble it like a puzzle.

Knowing the pain and trauma associated with various surgeries, we had an underlying fear of one of our children having to endure something similar. The thought of Emma undergoing this hellish surgery almost burned through my ability to cope. I could not call Tracey in Florida and tell her, as I didn't want her to worry while she was away. She would be home in a couple of days, so I just waited with Emma and held her close, praying for God to heal her.

It is often said that there is no bond like that between a mother and child. It is equally true that there is no power like a father's love for his child. On the night before Tracey was due to come back home, Emma was sleeping in her crib and I went into her room to check on her. Lying peacefully on her back, I just stared at her, trying to comprehend not only this looming problem but also awed by the love I felt for my youngest daughter.

I was suddenly seized by the need to pray for her yet again. This time I placed my hand on her forehead—on the area that was so pronounced—and asked Jesus to heal her, just as He healed others when He walked the earth.

As I prayed I felt a slow and gentle warmth flow through my body and intensify in my hand as I suddenly felt a slight movement under my palm, directly over the swollen area of Emma's head. I wasn't sure what I was feeling, and rather than reflexively move my hand away, I held it still. The movement grew stronger, like someone was tracing their finger under my palm. I was completely mesmerized, almost not believing what I was feeling. But it was unmistakable. After it stopped, I slowly withdrew my hand, looking for any sign that would explain what I had just felt, but Emma continued to lie still, sleeping peacefully.

There was no visible difference on her head at that moment, but I was overwhelmed by the power that had surged through my body and extended through my hand. A deep sense of awe and peace swept over me and persisted. The agonizing worry I had felt over the last few days vanished, and from that point on I had a great confidence that everything would be *all right*. Tracey returned home and we scheduled an appointment with the pediatric neurosurgeon.

My mom stopped by a few days after Tracey came home, and when she looked in on Emma said, "I might be crazy, but her head doesn't look nearly as bad as it did just last week."

Tracey and I exchanged knowing glances, and I told my mom about what I had felt while praying for Emma. Mom smiled and said, "Well, something must have happened because she sure looks better than she did last week."

Two weeks later, we took Emma to see the pediatric neurologist. He gave Emma a full exam, took careful measurements, ordered a CT scan, and scheduled a return appointment for one week after the scan. His conclusion at the follow-up appointment was quite reassuring. Although he found a slight asymmetry, his exam and the CT showed no evidence of craniosynostosis. Our relief was surpassed only by the thanks we gave to God.

I've never had the angelic experiences that Tracey has, and while I'm confident her faith would be as strong without them, the certainty of the angelic visits she witnessed must be reassuring. Regardless, we must accept many things on faith alone. I did not see the angel that Tracey saw in Nebraska, but I saw the aftereffect in the glow on her face, so although I cannot prove she saw an angel, I *know* she saw an angel. Similarly, although I cannot prove that what happened in Emma's room the night I laid my hand on her head and prayed for her was divine healing, I *know* that Jesus, working through the Holy Spirit, healed Emma that night.

There are no other reasonable explanations and there are no coincidences. I had not been predisposed to expect a healing of Emma's type. When I prayed, it was more of an expectation that there would be a slow and certain healing over time. I am convinced that the warmth I felt was the Holy Spirit moving through my body as Emma was healed. And in the days following that event, we noticed that the protrusion on Emma's forehead appeared to recede. When we finally saw the neurosurgeon, the discrepancy between her right and left sides was almost nonexistent.

Our God is an awesome God.

18

When the Doves Cried

The two years immediately following Emma's birth were joyous ones for us. We were a happy family of five, and other than the initial concerns for Emma, our lives seemed remarkably free of any strife. Tracey's parents, Tom and Mary, had moved back to Wisconsin, and Tracey thoroughly enjoyed them living nearby again. Repeated tests showed I was still free of hepatitis; Emma was growing into a happy, healthy toddler; Rebekah was a happy-go-lucky little schoolgirl; and Meghan was coming into her own as a bright, beautiful teenager as she transitioned from middle school to high school.

In the fall of 2002, Tom had a small stroke that affected his balance. Even after he recovered, he began to stumble and his gait was unsteady. Not long after that, Mary's health began to deteriorate. From that time on, they walked almost hand in hand in what would become a long good-bye over the next two years. Tom's problems seemed almost minor compared to Mary's. By October, Mary was experiencing bouts of fatigue, chest pain, and prolonged episodes of shortness of breath. Test indicated she was suffering from an empyema—an infection in the area of her lung-cancer surgery.

With Tom and Mary both in their seventies, even minor health issues could be exhausting—and Mary's were far from minor. She had surgery to remove the infected tissue in her lung, and the healing treatment required care in a rehabilitation hospital.

Tracey's father could not live by himself. So early in November Tom moved in with us. He used a walker to aid his mobility and his speech was noticeably slurred. Invisible strokes, too small to be detected, were occurring, and their toll was clearly noticeable.

Mary had healed enough to join us at our home in mid-December. She still required daily wound care, so moving to their home was not yet an option. As winter slowly turned to spring, they had both stabilized and insisted on moving back to their own home in May. Tom now needed a scooter to remain mobile and his voice was nearly inaudible. It was a bitter pill for a man who once depended on his voice, in sales, for his livelihood. He was a brilliant conversationalist.

Their move came just as another crisis befell Mary—further checkups revealed that she had breast cancer. She had a mastectomy in June, followed by chemotherapy. Her illnesses seemed to claim her body piece by piece. Just as Mary was recovering from her cancer surgery and treatment, Tom's health declined even more precipitously and the family began an almost around-the-clock vigil to be at Tom and Mary's side. With Tracey and Leslie-Ann living within a few miles of them, their efforts were now spelled by visits from the rest of the siblings—Susie, Tom, and Rob—which grew in frequency and duration over the next several months.

By fall 2003 Tom was almost entirely homebound. His last venture outside the home, other than hospital visits, was in late August. Shortly afterward, he developed a severe kidney infection that seemed as if it would claim his life. During his hospitalization, Mary was home alone and fell while going out to get the mail, breaking her hip. As the days grew shorter, so did our hope that we would see another Christmas with Tom and Mary. However, neither were ready to give up. They both rallied and were home by Thanksgiving.

Both survived for another enjoyable Christmas with the entire family—and though no one spoke of it, it was clear this would be their last. Each moment spent together was more precious, each meal savored a little more, each laugh a bit heartier, and every smile a little brighter throughout our final Christmas together.

As our watch continued through an icy winter, Tom was losing his fight, though not his will, to hang on. One particular night, as Tracey sat with Tom while he was sleeping, she suddenly felt a presence stirring within her father—an incredible peace seemed to envelop them both. Looking at Tom and seeing he was awake, Tracey asked, "Dad, I know you can't talk, but just blink once for yes and twice for no—are there angels here with you now?" Very purposefully, and looking directly at Tracey, he blinked hard, one time only, and smiled broadly at her.

Tracey knew the end was near. Then on February 18, 2004, with the entire family gathered at his side, her father finally eased his grip on this life and went to be with the Lord.

Tom's final gift to Tracey was a "hug," and it came in a most unexpected way. Though not unanticipated, the finality of Tom's death and especially the sound of his last gasp for breath startled everyone in the room. As Tracey saw her dad leaving, she stood and shouted, "Dad!" In the next instant, she felt an intense warm rush—the unmistakable feeling of her dad's soul moving through her, connecting with every fiber of her being. She could feel his love—as though she were breathing in his very essence—even his scent. It was so overpowering, she collapsed on the couch behind her.

She was certain she and her father had just embraced each other, but she was a bit overwhelmed and bewildered by her experience. Not wanting to intrude on or overshadow the rest of the family's mourning, she waited until Father Peter and Deacon Ellen from St. Francis church arrived before she uttered a word of her experience.

These faithful ones had ministered to Tom and Mary throughout their long illnesses, and it didn't take them long to arrive. After attending to their official duties and praying with the family, Tracey took Father Peter aside and, struggling to describe what had happened, told him the sequence of events and her feelings as best she could. Having served a number of years in hospice, he was quite familiar with the process of death and dying, and Father Peter nodded knowingly—flashing his warm, reassuring smile.

The situation and feelings Tracey described seemed not to surprise him at all. He had seen or talked to many other family members who had shared similar experiences. In his estimation, as a departed soul journeys on, they sometimes pass through or near the soul of a loved one left behind. That one will often feel a brief connection—and it was the fleeting communion of their souls that Tracey felt so strongly. When she finds that she is missing her dad most deeply, she thinks back to that time and is greatly comforted by the warmth of his "embrace."

The next few days were a blur of grief, preparation, and remembrance as we readied for Tom's funeral. Mary was a mere shell of herself. When Tom died it was as if Mary's zest for life, her *raison d'être*, had suddenly vanished, so the family did their best to rally around her and keep her spirits up. The day of the funeral was a typically crisp, cold February day as we gathered at St. Francis for our final good-byes and the celebration of Tom's wonderful life. It was a beautiful service, replete with memories read by each of their children, and even the grandchildren. Meghan and Rebekah each read something special that they wanted to say at their grandpa's funeral and so contributed to the endearing farewell.

At the close of the service, I took my position with the pallbearers to wheel Tom's casket down the aisle. Suddenly a stirring rendition of "Amazing Grace" erupted from the instrument of a flawless bagpiper. The cacophonous tones resonated within the church and filled our hearts. Most every eye glistened with tears.

As I entered our vehicle to warm it up for the family, my mind was flooded with memories of Tom and my concern for

Mary, Tracey, and our girls. Rebekah, in particular, seemed almost inconsolable during the funeral. Only ten years old, she was overwhelmed by the heartache and loss she obviously felt. Meghan was fifteen, and though she had always been close to Tom, so connected early on, her spirituality and deep convictions lent her the certainty of Tom's place with the Lord. Their cousin Emily would also be riding with us, and she held tightly to the same faith as Meghan.

Still, the sadness of Tom's parting permeated us to our core and left us with a chill as cold as the winter air. I knew the mood in the car would be heavy, and I was all out of words to assuage the girls' grief. I was struggling with my own emotions, trying to find a way to say something that might help.

As I started the Suburban, I heard an odd sound that seemed to come from everywhere and nowhere in particular. At first, I refused to believe what I might be hearing. It seemed to be coming from the engine—maybe a loose fan belt? I turned down the radio and listened more carefully. Then I turned off the engine; the sound was still there but I could not determine its exact location. It was a familiar sound, comforting and soothing. Just for a moment, I sat in the stillness and let the gentle sound fill me up.

As Meghan and Emily entered the car, I simply asked if they heard a noise. They both acknowledged the same sound I was hearing. It was the comforting, unmistakable cooing of a mourning dove!

Disbelieving my own ears and wanting to prove to myself that it was real, I turned the engine on and off again. I turned the radio on and off as well, and then we looked under every seat, in every compartment, even on the roof. I opened the hood to see if a cat had climbed in to warm itself—nothing. The dove still cooed.

I'm outside every day. We have several bird feeders, and doves sit on our chimney, their calls echoing down our fireplace and filling the house—I know the call of a dove. There is no other explanation for the sound we heard in our Suburban after Tom's funeral. The wonderment and thrill we felt as we heard the dove were equally real. In fact, the cry stayed with us all the way to the cemetery, comforting us as we prepared to lay Tom to rest. Emily and Meghan sat mesmerized during the short journey.

Having exhausted all other possibilities and finally believing what my ears were telling me, I knew this had to be a message carried by angels, perhaps the Holy Spirit himself, to let us know that Tom was at peace. He was with the Lord, and we should indeed celebrate his life rather than mourn our loss.

With Tom's death, half the embers that stoked the fires of Tom and Mary's love for each other had gone cold. Mary's previous slow decline hastened. Tracey often refers to the night her dad died as the moment her mom began to leave as well.

Over the course of the next several months, Mary's life became a series of doctor visits, hospital stays, and long days at home in bed. By late summer 2004, Mary had been diagnosed with cirrhosis and her energy was almost nonexistent. It was bitterly ironic that Mary, a lifelong teetotaler, would meet her demise as the result of cirrhosis. Mary managed to hang on until just after Thanksgiving, passing on November 29, 2004. The end came rather swiftly. Though nothing had appeared to change in those last few weeks, on the Friday before she died, the housekeeper said good-bye to Mary and "I'll see you next week!" Mary replied, "No you won't" and flashed a coy smile back at her. Certainly she must have known.

On a gray December 2, we again filled St. Francis church for what seemed like a surreal *déjà vu,* yet filled with far too much pain to be an illusion. Virtually all of the same people gathered in the same pews. Even Father Peter's sermon seemed familiar—Tom and Mary's life so intertwined it was difficult to eulogize one without honoring the other. The same pall-bearers bore the casket down the aisle, and the same version of "Amazing Grace" reverberated from the bagpipes.

Even the icy air was familiar as we walked out of the church. It seemed as though we hadn't quite left Tom's funeral nine months earlier, and now with Mary's, the long journey was finally over.

This time as we headed to the cemetery, I drove alone. Rebekah and Emma stayed back at the church with my parents. Meghan and Emily went with their cousin Erin, Leslie-Ann's daughter, and her future husband, Greg.

As Mary's three eldest granddaughters piled into Greg's Subaru and readied themselves for the short journey to the cemetery, an oddly familiar sound gently filled the interior of the car. Meghan and Emily recognized it immediately; the dove's cries had returned! Meghan said it was the most haunting yet comforting sound she has ever heard. Emily said she and Meghan just looked at each other in disbelief. With tears streaming down their faces, they told Erin and Greg they had heard the dove nine months earlier after Tom's funeral.

This could not be a coincidence. Not only did Meghan and Emily hear the same sound as we'd heard before, this time there were two different witnesses to the cooing of the dove. Erin and Greg heard it as well.

To reinforce the veracity of this event, Greg had never met Tom and only met Mary a few times. He never really knew either of them well enough to become grief-stricken. He identifies himself as an agnostic, in fact, and is certainly not given to what some might interpret as religious hysteria. He heard the second dove as distinctly as the others.

The meaning and message are clear. For Christians, the dove symbolizes the Holy Spirit. Universally, the dove is recognized as the symbol of peace and of hope, and two doves together represent love and fidelity—completing the circle and the bond between Mary and Tom, even in their passing, and giving all of us the message that they are together with the Lord, in His most perfect love.

19

When Angels Whisper and Shout

We have been awed by many other incidents where we perceived that God used His heavenly angels to intervene directly in our lives—in ways both overt and subtle.

Soon after we returned home to Wisconsin in 1990, one of Tracey's best friends, Caroline, died of breast cancer. Several months after her death, Tracey stopped by her grave site one evening to visit. Caroline is buried at one of the Milwaukee area's largest cemeteries. The gates lead to secluded, expansive grounds that are heavily wooded and very private—a virtual world away from the busy traffic and hectic lives just beyond the steel fence that ensconces the quiet resting-place of thousands.

After finding Caroline's marker near an expanse of towering maple trees, Tracey parked her car and sat on a nearby bench. She was thankful to be alone with Caroline, with only the trees to accompany her—swaying and sighing in the evening breeze.

Lost in her thoughts, Tracey barely noticed when another car came to a halt on a parallel road nearly one hundred feet away. Though she saw two men get out of the car, she did not register a hint of concern when they failed to go directly to any nearby grave site. She scarcely noted that they split up and moved in opposite directions away from their car, parallel to the road on which they had parked.

As Tracey sat in quiet reflection, she suddenly heard a man shout, "Tracey, leave!" Initially not perceiving the warning implicit in the message, she looked up, wondering who had recognized her. Then she noticed the two men who had parked nearby several minutes earlier. They had indeed split up and were now walking toward her, coming from opposite sides.

Still not quite perceiving the inherent danger of her situation, she just looked past the men and again wondered who had called her name. Now just fifty or sixty feet away, suddenly Tracey heard the same voice in a louder and more urgent tone: "Tracey, leave NOW!" With that stern command, she leapt to her feet and covered the short distance to her car, less than fifteen feet away. She got in and sped off just as the men closed in.

Tracey was at first confused by what had just happened, but as she passed the gates of the cemetery on her way out, she was clearly shaken by the event.

Even a casual look at the circumstances yields no other conclusion—near dusk, two men slowly stalked Tracey in a deserted cemetery. Lost in her own thoughts, as they approached and the danger grew, she suddenly heard a commanding male voice telling her to leave. She had earlier scanned the area and was convinced she was alone. If she was not alone and someone had been watching her, who knew her name, why would he not directly show himself to stop the advance of the two men? Further, if someone had been watching these events unfold, why would the men not flee, or at least hesitate at the sound of the voice? I could go through many different scenarios, but there is only one conclusion: An angel was watching over Tracey, protecting her.

We have had several other events that have revealed God's love and presence in our lives. While God sometimes intervenes when we least expect it, He also responds to our prayers and comes when we call Him and need Him most.

Faithful prayer has its own power. We were reminded of this with two dramatic incidents that arose during our 2002 trip to Yellowstone and Jackson Hole, Wyoming.

After a meandering journey where we spent several days on the road, interspersed with visits to Tracey's aunt, cousins, and the Vandersnicks in Nebraska, we arrived in Jackson Hole late on a Sunday night in mid-August. After we settled in to the condo we had rented, Meghan and I headed in to town to get groceries for our stay over the next week.

The grocery store was about ten miles away, and we arrived just before the store closed and were among the last few customers to leave. As we loaded the groceries into our van in what was now the middle of a darkening parking lot, we were in somewhat of a hurry to get back to Tracey, Rebekah, and Emma—knowing they were hungry and anxious for us to return.

As Meghan and I settled into the van, I turned the key in the ignition and—nothing! No lights, not even a click from the starter. I tried all the standard procedures—checked the battery and cables, the shift lever, the starter—everything I could think of, to no avail.

I tried turning the key a few more times and still no response—no grinding, clicking, not the slightest hint of power. Meghan, who was fourteen at the time, was looking more and more panicked. I told her not to worry, took her hand, and said that God would take care of us. I said a brief prayer. "God, we're here in Jackson Hole and our car won't start. No matter what is wrong, I know you can fix it. We ask in Jesus' name that you please let it start tonight and get us back to Tracey and the girls."

I looked at Meghan, put the key in the ignition, twisted it forward—and the engine roared to life. I will never forget Meghan's face as she exclaimed, "That was awesome!" For as long as we owned that van, we never had that problem again.

While this event did not hold the same drama as others did, I think it highlights that if we faithfully ask the Lord for His help, we might get exactly what we need—no matter how small or great. Moreover, it was a great example for Meghan to witness the power of faithful prayer.

Another incident during that same vacation was so unexpected, dramatic, and unmistakably effected by the hand of God that it is seared in my memory. While traveling home on the final leg of our trip through Minnesota on I-90, dusk was gathering and traffic was incredibly busy and fast. That and what seemed like thousands of bugs smearing on our windshield made it difficult to see—all making me nervous. Given our previous experiences, we were always a bit on edge when we traveled, especially in an unfamiliar area.

We typically hold hands and ask the Lord to bless and protect us before we hit the road. Even though we had already prayed earlier in the day, I was becoming increasingly anxious on this stretch of freeway, so I asked Tracey and the girls to hold hands, and we said another quick prayer, asking the Lord to watch over us and protect us.

What happened next is inexplicable and surreal. Less than a minute after our prayer, maybe seconds, a doe suddenly appeared less than fifty feet in front of our van. We were moving at 75 miles per hour. Somehow I missed hitting her, but *how* I avoided her is the mystery.

The deer appeared so quickly, I had no time to react. Before I knew it, and without any apparent effort on my part, our van simply glided around the doe, which seemed frozen in place. I've had other occasions in which I have used high-speed maneuvers to avoid cars or other obstacles in my way. I once did this to avoid a car that suddenly pulled in front of me while I was traveling at 55 miles per hour. In that instance, as I jerked the steering wheel with two quick half-turns, first to the left and then quickly back to the right, *everything* in the car flew around me, including the hot coffee that splashed everywhere. On this occasion, while traveling at 75 miles per hour in a top-heavy GMC Safari van with my family and our luggage packed all around us, there wasn't a hint of turbulence or violent action within the car—I don't think the girls even looked up.

Tracey just looked at me with eyes wide. "How did you miss that deer?"

I was so stunned, even bewildered, I could only stammer, "I, I, I . . . don't know." I then answered her question with one of my own, "What just happened?" And then another, "Did you see that?"

I would like to say I had the wits and reaction to save us from almost certain disaster. It would be easier to explain, and I would have been somewhat of a hero in the eyes of my family. But the deer was too close to avoid—so close that I could clearly see her eyes and the details of her face, even the twitching of her nostrils. I'm a hunter and outdoorsman, quite familiar with deer and a good judge of distances. There is no possible way I could have missed her, moving at 75 miles per hour—at least no possible human way. At that speed, I would have covered the distance in less than half a second.

I can only describe it this way: It felt very much like a giant hand gently cradled us and guided our van around that deer. To this day I have no recollection of having moved the steering wheel even a fraction of an inch to avoid her—I never even touched the brakes.

In the next few seconds, it dawned on us exactly what had happened—our sideways glances and small smiles spoke clearly to us, without any words between us—we just knew. Later that evening, as we tucked the girls into bed at the hotel, we gave thanks to God and hugged each other a little bit harder, thankful for God's watchful eye.

Another hint of the Lord's presence happened on a somewhat spontaneous trip to Florida in 2004, over spring break, to visit Tracey's sister Susie and her husband, Dave, at their beach home in Melbourne, Florida.

On our trip home, we stayed overnight at a hotel in Tennessee. The next morning Tracey, Meghan, and Rebekah got ready for the day and let Emma and me sleep in a bit. They went downstairs to get themselves some juice and muffins and a cup of coffee for me.

As Tracey sat with the girls while they ate their breakfast, an older gentleman suddenly walked up to the table and asked if he could sit down with them. Tracey was surprised, since more than enough tables were open. He didn't have any food or drink with him, but there was something oddly comforting and disarming about this man, and Tracey readily agreed to his request. Tracey and Meghan both recall his deep blue and sparkling, almost playful eyes. Then, in a series of questions and comments, he made it obvious that he knew details about Tracey and the girls that would be virtually impossible for a stranger to know or guess. Somehow he knew our family.

He looked at Meghan and said, "You must play basketball, probably two guard." That is the exact position Meghan always played. "You look like you have a good arm; I'll bet you play softball, too." He then added with a wry smile, "You probably play third base and catcher, because you need to have a good arm to play those positions." Although Meghan is small, she's always been athletic and quite strong. To guess that she played catcher would have been a bit of a stretch. She wasn't wearing athletic gear of any kind that would give away her interests. In fact, she was still wearing her pajamas because we had at least ten hours of driving ahead of us.

The stranger then looked at Rebekah, who was ten years old, and said, "Do you like being a big sister?" Rebekah nodded. Emma was not with them, so for him to guess that she had a younger sister was more than random.

He turned to Tracey, and with a warm, broad smile asked, "Did you enjoy your Florida vacation?" Enthralled by this visit from what she knew in her heart must be an angel, and almost giggling with delight, she just answered with a simple nod of her head and a yes. He asked, "Do you have a long way to go yet?" Tracey told him that we still had many hours ahead of us on our way back to Wisconsin. He rose, and with his eyes still sparkling, left them with these words: "Well, I'm sure you will have a safe trip. May God bless you!" And with that, he walked quickly out of the room and disappeared behind a small group of people waiting at the front desk.

Tracey and Meghan just looked at each other and smiled— they both knew exactly what had just happened. In fact, they knew the moment he sat down, and Tracey silently mouthed to Meghan, *Angel!*

When they returned to our room with my coffee, their beaming faces and animated gestures nearly belied the first words out of their mouths: "We just saw an angel!" I believe this was another whisper from God, His way of letting us know that He was with us and watching over us.

20

Of Fires, Fate, and Faith

The word *fire* appears in the Bible over six hundred times. Perhaps no other word in the Bible has so many symbolic and disparate meanings. It is consuming, sustaining, terrifying, comforting, holy, punishing, and sanctifying. For Tracey and me, such have been the fires in our life together.

Undoubtedly, the pivotal point in our lives was the car crash that changed so much for us. It pushed us so violently and completely from our expected path that it forced a dramatic new reality upon us. In our case, it seemed almost entirely based upon the decisions of someone else—the drunk driver who hit us. We had no other choice than to endure its life-altering consequences.

Whether or not anything in our past could have made a difference to change exactly when and where we were on the night of the collision I will never know. What I do know is that the driver who hit us made his own choices that night that forever changed everything about our world. The intersection of his decisions and our presence collided on the road, and his future ended where ours began.

Tracey and I sometimes wonder what our lives would have been like were it not for those events so long ago. However, even acknowledging how different our lives are, we cannot say with certainty that our lives would have been any better had it never happened. Logically, it would seem that if we did not have the physical and mental challenges we now endure, our lives would be easier.

Through the trauma of the wreck that exploded on the highway that night to the months and years of recovery and our daily struggle to triumph over its everlasting effects, our lives have been an incredible journey.

Our life is a study in contrasts. How do we reconcile the agony of injury, pain, and disability against the ecstasy of God's love, redemption, and peace—all in a single moment? How do we live with fear and faith borne in that same instant? This is the dichotomy that still exists in our lives—the peace that Tracey felt in her near-death experience against the sheer panic and horror of the crash itself still follows us in one form or another.

We have endured great sacrifice but also have great blessings that continue to color our lives since that agonizing night. The dark palette of fear, pain, and regret has stained the brilliant tapestry of our lives painted by the simple grace of humanity, the love of family and friends, and the transcendent beauty and rich blessings that can only come from God himself. Answers may not always be obvious, so we rely on God to bless us with His guidance—and where there is darkness, we rely on Him for light.

What if we had sailed right through that moment in time without the crash? What would life have been then? No one but God can say if it would have been better.

Tracey and I have had to meet and overcome challenges far beyond what could be reasonably expected of one couple. Every stress and strain, each trial, is a ready source of fuel for the burning fuse of distress that was set off by our crash so long ago. Each flare threatens to immolate us.

Obviously, the crash has had lifelong consequences for us in so many ways. The ever-present pain is exhausting. Some days, Tracey's arthritis is so bad she can barely walk and her mornings are an exercise in near torture. Each step feels like she is grinding shards of glass through her ankle, knees, and hip. My joints do not hurt me nearly as much as Tracey's. My pain is more diffused—at times pulsating throughout my body like waves. Tracey also struggles with post-traumatic peripheral neuropathy, which is debilitating and painful. No matter how much we fight, we cannot seem to escape the effects of the crash.

As we look past the darkest edges of our life, we know that God has brushed our lives with the richness of His blessings. And I know that however painful and difficult things may be for us, God has intervened and used what happened to us for many other positive outcomes that may never have occurred without the pain.

We can't, and won't, dwell on what might have been. I'm thankful I'm here, thankful to still have Tracey, and thankful for the many blessings we've received since. In the end, we can't change anything; we can only acknowledge that perhaps we were right where we were supposed to be.

That we have had incredible experiences in our lives there can be no doubt. I don't know why we've had to endure so many hardships, but I know there's a reason Tracey said what she did during our ride back to La Crosse so many years ago: "You and I should get to know each other better."

More than anything else, that incident reminds me time after time of the surety and strength of our bond and the abiding promise of God's love. We were brought together by God, and through all that we have endured, I know He has a purpose and plan for our lives together—and that is enough for us to weather all that life has thrown at us.

Like any parents, our most glaring vulnerability is the welfare of our children. We were reminded of this again as we saw Meghan struggle with health issues during her junior year in high school. Always a standout athlete, especially in softball, she missed almost her entire season due to severe pain in her hips, back, and legs. Her pain waxed and waned over the next few years, but by her sophomore year in college, Meghan began having pain so severe that no amount of medication or therapy effectively diminished it in any way. Even simple movements like turning over in bed, much less walking, were torturous—the pain searing through her body like a branding iron.

After dozens of doctor visits, she was finally diagnosed with the autoimmune disorder ankylosing spondylitis (AS). This disorder is essentially rheumatoid arthritis of the spine and sacroiliac joint. The same genetic defect that causes AS also causes ulcerative colitis, from which Meghan also suffers. She was truly miserable. Watching Meghan suffer over the past years has been heartbreaking for us, but she relies on powerful medication to control her symptoms and on God for strength.

We now find ourselves in the midst of one of our most trying times. There is an economic firestorm sweeping through the U.S. and the entire world, and our family has not been immune to these problems. Like many others, I lost my job. In fact, as of this writing, I have lost two jobs in the past three years.

We cannot control every event in our life, but we can control how we respond. Tracey and I look to God for strength and guidance, and we turn to each other for love and support. I am not a Pollyanna (a completely irrational optimist). I don't pretend that we haven't had tremendous challenges in our life or try to ignore or wish them away—I acknowledge them and do my best to cope as they come along. Mostly, I recognize and focus on the blessings that balance everything out. I don't think our troubles are given to us by God, but if He has any hand in our trials, I believe He can and does use even the most painful events in our lives for a greater purpose.

In writing this book, it has occurred to me that the overriding theme of our life story is not the troubles and challenges we have faced, or even how we have responded, but God's abiding love. At every difficult point in our lives, we have felt God's presence and His love in a special way.

When we were too exhausted, scared, or traumatized to carry on, it was God's love that rescued us and lifted us up to see another day. I can truly say that in every crisis in our lives, God has provided perhaps not always what we wanted, but in every instance exactly what we needed. His love has sustained us again and again. God loves us and reveals himself to us through Jesus Christ, whom we have accepted as our Savior and Lord—it really is that simple.

Tracey and I have had countless people comment on how well we handle the difficulties we've faced and yet still manage to maintain an upbeat, positive attitude. It's not always easy, but the alternative is to live darkly, with little hope and almost no joy—so no thank you. The trials of today merely lay the groundwork for the triumphs of tomorrow. Though we are still in the midst of yet another difficult struggle as I write these pages, I hear whispers of God's promises for a better day and I feel His guiding hand in our lives.

With incredible highs and lows throughout our roller-coaster life, our faith journey has sometimes followed the same jagged course. Sometimes our faith has been strongest when we felt the farthest from God; at other times when we were perhaps most complacent, we would suddenly feel God's hand guiding us yet again—sparking a resurgence that would again see our faith soar to new heights.

One such occurrence came to me while we were visiting Tom and Mary on an extended vacation in Florida during the winter of 1994. They had returned to Florida after Christmas, where Mary was still recovering from her cancer surgeries and treatments. We were not only eager to see Tom and Mary again, but we had also scheduled follow-up visits with several physicians and the attorney whom our families had hired to oversee our numerous medical expenses, bills, and insurance claims. This would be our final trip to put closure on the many loose ends that remained.

Even as it seemed we had finally found some peace in our lives following Rebekah's birth and Mary's healing and recovery from her cancer, I found a growing sense of restlessness and unease rising within me. While our appointments highlighted the vast strides we had made in our overall recovery, they also served as vivid reminders of the damage we had incurred. This flood of memories came at a particularly vulnerable time for me. Numerous sinus infections left me with constant headaches and growing fatigue, and I began to question my long-term ability to stay healthy, work, and provide financial security for my family.

We were staying at Tom and Mary's during our visit, and as I tried to get six-month-old Rebekah settled down to sleep one evening, I decided to take her for a walk in her stroller, hoping the rhythmic motion would help. As we walked on through the night's cool breezes, Rebekah's long sighs finally signaled her surrender to sleep's gentle hold and I turned my thoughts to God's endless wisdom.

I found myself pouring out to God my deepest fears and worries about our future. Despite my determined efforts to maintain an unyielding belief in His provision, I confessed to God my fracturing faith—almost ashamed of my weakness.

I had been engaged in silent conversation with God for several minutes, my walk lasting longer than anticipated, when a sudden stillness fell upon me and my thoughts and worries quieted. What happened next can only be described as the most intense connectedness with God I had ever experienced. I certainly felt God's hand and presence in the hospital after our crash, in His answers to so many of my prayers, seeing Tracey's shining face after Beth and Chris's funeral, seeing Emma revived after her difficult birth, in the soft cooing of the doves after Tom and Mary's funerals, and when I felt His fingers beneath my outstretched hand as He healed Emma's head. All of those events paled in comparison to that night as I felt God's peace and love descend upon me, almost consuming me.

Though God did not speak words aloud to me, the unmistakable message was "Be still, and know that I am God," and, to paraphrase Scripture, "Let tomorrow worry about tomorrow—I will always be here, and I will always provide for you."

Earthly words cannot convey the profound peace and comfort that filled every cell of my being. I've had a lifetime of incredible experiences and seen amazing highs and lows, but nothing, absolutely nothing, compares to the peace, love, and sheer joy I experienced that night. If those feelings are even a hint of what Tracey experienced with Jesus after she "died" in our crash, then truly I understand her comfort with death and her longing to be with the Lord again—someday.

From the quiet street of that long ago night until this very day, I have walked with that promise through all of my days. In every difficulty, when I find within me a dark well of despair and fear, I dip my cup of faith into the promise of that night and find it overflowing with hope—and I am renewed.

Some have suggested that perhaps the devil himself has laid troubles in our path to destroy our hope, break the bonds of our marriage, or draw us away from God. If I accept that God has a personal interest in our lives, then I cannot deny that Satan may seek to destroy what God has done. If that is true, then the enemy has failed miserably.

Not only are Tracey and I stronger than ever, our trials have served only to strengthen our bond with the Lord. Every fire that has threatened to consume us has only purified our lives and tempered our faith to make it stronger and more durable. God has taken each of our burdens and turned them into incredible blessings. Surrendering to God is not giving up. Rather, it is an invitation for Him to work His will through us, no matter what shape that may take. Actually, surrendering to His will is the greatest freedom we can ever experience.

Tracey and I are no more spiritually gifted, or certainly any more loved by God than anyone else. I cannot explain why we have had the angelic and miraculous experiences in our lives. Perhaps our faith has allowed us greater recognition of these events as they have unfolded in our lives, but that does not mean we are more likely than any other person to experience God's benevolence and grace. There is nothing special about us. As Tracey says, "We are all special to God, and anything that has happened to me can happen to anyone."

Even with Tracey's near-death experience and the visit by the angel who touched her as she lay on the road that night, she doesn't feel she was specially prepared or specifically chosen for that event or any other experience. At the time of our accident, she had always had a relationship with Christ, but in her own words, she had "never been overly disciplined about my beliefs. I believed, and that was always enough." She had never really thought about angels before the accident and, other than their biblical appearances, held no opinion as to whether they existed or not. The miracles and blessings we have received, whether through angels or other manifestations, all come from God. We don't worship angels; we worship God. God makes himself known through many means—angels are just one.

If I can offer one thing to the person out there who is desperately seeking some sign of God in their own life, it is this: Keep your eyes and ears open at all times—watch and listen with a faithful heart. God is with you always and working wonders and miracles, for you alone, on an almost daily basis. Be ready and open to His works and He will reveal himself in ways great and small.

Most of God's miracles are not as dramatic as Emma's sudden healing or as breathtaking as Tracey's angelic encounters. Rather, they are the small events that whisper themselves to us nearly every day, where God reveals himself to us not in one blinding flash but in the unexpected hug from a friend at an especially needful time, the extra cash at exactly the right moment, the comforting kindness from a "stranger" with a warm smile on an otherwise difficult day, the "coincidence" that keeps us safe from what seems like certain harm, or the sudden insight and wisdom that comes in response to a problem that has been especially troubling.

Faith is its own reward, God's love is real, and He is the answer in our deepest trials. Jesus is the way to God, and the Holy Spirit ensures God's presence with us always. There is greater glory to be had from our difficulties than we can sometimes understand.

I do hope readers find inspiration from our story, gain insight into their own struggles, and know that the trials of this life are but fleeting compared to God's abiding love.

May you find in God the peace that surpasses all understanding.

Our daughters, Meghan, Rebekah,
and Emma (top to bottom),
on a trip to Colorado, 2003

Meghan's wedding in 2011. Me and Tracey, Meghan and Jordan, and Emma and Rebekah. Photo by Lisa Matthewson.

Tracey and me, 2012

Acknowledgments

Thank you to my literary agent, Mary Sue Seymour; an agent has only her reputation at stake when agreeing to represent a book. I am so grateful she took a risk on me and this book.

Deep gratitude to Bethany House for the amazing efforts of their staff in bringing my book to publication. Tim Peterson not only took a chance on this rough gem, but expertly shaped it into something others could appreciate. His guidance and care cannot be understated. Thank you also to Jeff Braun for his extensive polishing of the many different facets, allowing them to truly shine. And many thanks to Nancy Renich for the final touches that made it a finished work.

Thank you to Paul Higdon for a truly compelling cover. Your vision and artistry are much appreciated.

Thank you to everyone in our Bible study group at North-brook Church in Richfield, Wisconsin. You prayed, and God granted! Your support is warmly appreciated.

To the many friends and family who guided and supported this process, thank you.

Special thanks to Tracey's sister Susan Gill, whose careful notes helped me to reconstruct so many details of those first days and weeks after our crash and also helped me find the heroes and other witnesses who were on the scene.

Words are inadequate to thank the heroes on the highway that stopped and risked their own lives so that we would have a fighting chance at ours. With all the gratitude I can muster, thank you!

Dann Stadler is an energetic speaker, author, father, husband, and tireless advocate for Christ. Creator and author of the popular website www.saturdayspromise.com, he encourages readers to live in Saturday's Promise, where the sins of our past are vanquished by the promise of Christ's resurrection. He and his family live in Jackson, Wisconsin. Learn more at www.saturdayspromise.com.